Language Curriculum Design and Socialisation

D1471665

Full details of all our publications can be found on http://www.multilingual-matters.com, or by writing to Multilingual Matters, St Nicholas House, 31–34 High Street, Bristol BS1 2AW, UK.

Language Curriculum Design and Socialisation

Peter Mickan

MULTILINGUAL MATTERS
Bristol • Buffalo • Toronto

To my family members for their support and reality checks

Library of Congress Cataloging in Publication Data
A catalog record for this book is available from the Library of Congress.
Mickan, Peter, author.
Language Curriculum Design and Socialisation/Peter Mickan.
Includes bibliographical references.
1. Language arts (Early childhood)–Curricula. 2. Language arts (Early childhood)–Social aspects. 3. Curriculum planning–Social aspects. 4. Socialization. 5. English language–Study and teaching (Early childhood)–Foreign speakers. I. Title.
LB1139.5.L35M53 2013
372.6–dc23 2012036453

British Library Cataloguing in Publication Data
A catalogue entry for this book is available from the British Library.

ISBN-13: 978-1-84769-830-8 (hbk)
ISBN-13: 978-1-84769-829-2 (pbk)

Multilingual Matters
UK: St Nicholas House, 31-34 High Street, Bristol BS1 2AW, UK.
USA: UTP, 2250 Military Road, Tonawanda, NY 14150, USA.
Canada: UTP, 5201 Dufferin Street, North York, Ontario M3H 5T8, Canada.

Channel View Publications
UK: St Nicholas House, 31-34 High Street, Bristol BS1 2AW, UK.
USA: UTP, 2250 Military Road, Tonawanda, NY 14150, USA.
Canada: UTP, 5201 Dufferin Street, North York, Ontario M3H 5T8, Canada.

The policy of Multilingual Matters/Channel View Publications is to use papers that are natural, renewable and recyclable products, made from wood grown in sustainable forests. In the manufacturing process of our books, and to further support our policy, preference is given to printers that have FSC and PEFC Chain of Custody certification. The FSC and/or PEFC logos will appear on those books where full certification has been granted to the printer concerned.

Typeset by R. J. Footring Ltd, Derby
Printed and bound in Great Britain by the MPG Books Group

… the process we are interested in is that of producing and understanding text in some context of situation, perhaps the most distinctive form of activity in the life of social man.
Halliday and Hasan (1985: 14)

Contents

Acknowledgements

I would like to thank colleagues and students who have encouraged research into language and learning. Colleagues include Garth Boomer, Christopher Candlin, David Nunan, Jill Burton and Peter Mühlhäusler. For the use of curriculum materials from the Adelaide Secondary School of English I thank the Principal, Julie Presser, and for permission to use the materials included from St Brigid's School my thanks to Bev. White and Bronwyn Custance. For assistance with editing and visuals in the text I wish to thank Jodie Martin, Hung Quoc Tran and Ralph Footring. Finally a special thanks to the energetic students and teachers in my applied linguistics research groups for the conversations and the challenges you have raised about language and learning in different contexts around the world.

Peter Mickan
Discipline of Linguistics
University of Adelaide
South Australia
August 2012

Preface

Language teaching and curriculum design have changed a lot over the last 50 years, from grammar-based, to functional-notional, to communicative, to task-based and more recently to genre-based. The designs have been based on linguistic, cognitive and more recently sociolinguistic theories of language and learning. The changes have increased the complexity of curricula as language educators have attempted to accommodate new insights into language and into language learning with the addition of new discourse, pragmatic and contextual elements.

This book fills a gap in language education through the application of social theory to curriculum design. The design views language as enmeshed in human activity, rather than as a system independent of non-linguistic phenomena. I have called it a social practice curriculum in order to represent language as integrated in people's social activity. The purpose is to provide a practical handbook on curriculum design which applies social theory to classroom practice.

The type of curriculum advocated in this book is constructed around the discourses or texts of social practices. Increasingly, texts and genres have been accepted as units of analysis for pedagogy (Christie & Martin, 2000; Cope & Kalantzis, 1993; Hyland, 2004a; Martin & Rose, 2005; Paltridge, 2001; Stillar, 1998; Swales, 1990). Texts integrate rather than segregate linguistic elements in social contexts (Harris, 1996; Mühlhäusler, 2003). Language is a significant meaning-making or semiotic resource (Halliday, 1978) for people's participation in social practices. We take part in communities with language structured as texts. The texts or discourses of social practices comprise the units of analysis for a curriculum. For example, the specific social practice I am engaged in at present is composing a preface to a book. This type of text is constructed with distinctive lexico-grammatical selections.

The aims of the book are:

- to provide teachers with a curriculum model for teaching children and adults in different contexts, from pre-school to adult education;

- to describe an integrated theoretical framework for curriculum design;
- to present exemplars of a text-based curriculum.

I have written this book as a practical guide for students, teachers, trainers and administrators with responsibilities for policy formulation and language planning. The curriculum design is readily adaptable to different educational systems and contexts. The text-based curriculum provides a structure that is flexible and user-friendly for teachers and a useful guide for learners. Texts are integral to our social practices and as such they imply teaching acts as well as offer materials for classroom tasks. They are integrated and holistic resources, ready for immediate use for short study tours and for programmes extending over years. The book includes examples of text-based curricula in order to illustrate the practical side of teaching with texts. The curriculum design offers options for centrally planned programmes as well as for teacher-initiated and locally developed courses. It is a design for planning language policies, teaching programmes and lesson activities. The book assumes a readership of native as well as non-native speakers of English. It is written for teachers and students (coursework and research) of English and other languages but the theory and design have application to education programmes in general.

Introduction: Curriculum Design and Renewal

There are very practical reasons for proposing a new curriculum model. National language policies in many countries, including Indonesia, Thailand, Taiwan and Korea, have extended the teaching of English into elementary school education and to students in secondary schools. For young children a traditional grammar-based curriculum is unsuitable. For older learners and for adults wishing to use languages in work or for study there is some urgency to learn to communicate. For them, progress in grammar-based approaches towards practical proficiency is irritatingly indirect and frustratingly slow. Alternative approaches to teaching, such as communicative language teaching and task-based teaching, retain a traditional analysis of grammar rather than a text-based analysis.

The curriculum design described in this book constructs the curriculum around social practices and their texts rather than presenting language as grammatical and lexical objects. Language use is integrated as texts for participation in social practices. Learners develop familiarity with texts from childhood, so they understand and relate to texts and their purposes. The ready availability of texts as resources for teaching simplifies curriculum planning and implementation. With texts, learners make meanings and extend their communicative resources for participation in language-based action. The design is adaptable to different circumstances, responsive to varied needs, and easy for teachers and administrators to use.

The reasons for renewing the language curriculum are many: large classes; heavy teacher workloads with minimal time for lesson preparation; the complexity of current curriculum models with multiple components such as functions and notions, grammatical forms, word lists as well as discourse features, learning strategies, learning processes and task types. National examinations perpetuate grammar-oriented pedagogies without supporting the use of language for real purposes. In many contexts, limited resources are allocated for the implementation of language policies and for further education of teachers.

There are also compelling pedagogical arguments. Productive pedagogies such as enquiry learning, problem-based learning, project learning and task-based teaching are having a significant impact on general education as educational planners strive to implement creative, challenging and exciting learning experiences for children. Educational authorities expect learners to engage in complex, problem-solving tasks, which second-language educators have regarded as beyond the language capacity of second-language learners, except at advanced levels. Language learners expect challenging and personally rewarding programmes in which they work together in a target language rather than act out artificial dialogues in simulated exercises.

There are pragmatic reasons for curriculum renewal. Education authorities mandate learning outcomes linked to graduates' effective participation in technologically globalised economies. Political pressure for accountability in education has spawned curriculum guidelines and assessment procedures that prescribe syllabuses and programme content. The need is for a tangible curriculum model to meet the challenges posed by global shifts in education and work, in which neighbours, workers and scholars need technical and personal discourse proficiencies rather than rote-learned speech.

It is the social character of language that forms the foundation of the curriculum model described in this book. Social theory offers an alternative to grammar-based teaching approaches. Instruction in this curriculum model is based on textual or discourse practices, with grammar analysed as a resource for making meanings. Learners work with and analyse language in use, integrated in texts.

Since the 1960s, language curricula have changed significantly. Grammatical syllabuses have been replaced by functional-notional, communicative, task-based and genre-based syllabuses. With each new approach the curriculum has become increasingly complex, with inclusion of functions and notions, task types, outcome statements, learning styles and preferences, learning and communication strategies, as well as genres and discourse features, added to traditional components of grammar, vocabulary, written exercises and comprehension questions.

The expanded curriculum has suited teachers working in ideal circumstances, with small, motivated classes, light teaching loads, and resource-rich classrooms, equipped with multimedia facilities. However, the fact is that the conditions for most language classes are not like this at all. More typical are large class sizes, minimally trained teachers, few resources, poorly equipped classrooms, duplicated materials instead of expensive textbooks and unmotivated students compelled by national policies to study languages. The enlarged curriculum has increased teachers' workloads and makes unrealistic demands based on complex language models and teaching frameworks.

Innovations in curriculum design and teaching approaches have had limited success in spearheading renewal of teaching and enhancement of learning. Despite new language policies and curriculum models in which communication has been set as an explicit goal, many learners study a language for years without enjoying the ability to communicate, whether joining in a discussion in class, working in a group or reading books for pleasure. In many classrooms, grammatical teaching and testing remain at centre stage, despite over four decades of promotion of communicative language teaching. In lessons, teachers struggle with the practicalities of student management, unsuitable resources, limited language skills and unrealistic teaching goals embodied in ambitious policy papers.

Curricula have changed from traditional, reductionist designs in which language is presented as discrete items of grammar and vocabulary to integrated skills in communication. Content-based programmes such as bilingual and immersion programmes exemplify language in action. In these programmes, learners work with the discourses or texts which constitute the content of subjects (Mickan, 2007). The approach is based on the belief that learning occurs through use, through making meanings and through participation in the ongoing tasks connected with teaching subjects, such as science or art or history. This replicates everyday language use, where it is integrated in social practices.

Texts are people's everyday experience of language: language used in contexts for social purposes. Social theory constructs a curriculum around the texts or discourses of social practices. Halliday (1985) describes texts as language in use. Our normal use of language is as texts in social action. Texts are cultural artefacts. They are semiotic resources upon which societies, communities and individuals depend for survival. Communities develop discourses for the performance and accomplishment of cultural activities. Language as text is systematically and fundamentally bound up with routines and specialised human activities. Significant human activities, or social practices, as I refer to them in this book, are carried out with language. Wordings are selected for the specific meanings associated with actual practices and are necessary for participation in the practices. The theory places meaning-making at the centre of teaching, with the analysis of the language system described as meaning potential. Lexico-grammatical elements from a language system are combined as texts for the expression of meanings. Instruction integrates lexico-grammatical analysis with learners' interpretations and expression of meanings. The intimate relationship between practices and texts is made transparent, by showing how language is used for organising and realising meanings.

We are able to observe in videos and DVDs and on iPhones how language and human activities are intimately connected in physical ecologies. Typically we use language together with visual, aural and material artefacts.

Language is embedded in human activity. From recordings of language we are able to observe and map patterns of language in action: the selections of wordings, which identify speakers and writers, situations, and purposes of conversations, of brochures and emails. The technology to record spoken texts, to store them in text banks and to make spoken texts visible with their component parts and patterns in transcripts and in printouts has opened up spoken language to detailed analysis. The electronic analysis of written texts with concordancing programmes gives insights into the intricacies of language variety, displaying patterns, changes and variations in language use, and revealing language as an open system responsive to transformations in changing environments, relationships and materials.

A social practice curriculum has significant advantages for foreign- and second-language instruction and courses in language for specific purposes. Education in schools centres on literacy learning and the development of new discourses and analytical skills connected with specialised subjects. Working with texts is what teachers in schools and universities do well. Although often criticised as inadequate contexts for language learning, in fact the situated talk and literacy activities in classrooms are tailored environments for building learners' discourse skills. This is also characteristic of academic teaching, as students learn the texts which constitute disciplinary studies. A second advantage is teachers' and learners' familiarity with texts in daily life. We grow up surrounded with texts in our social ecologies and we learn texts as part of normal socialisation. Teaching with texts builds upon learners' wide experiences of language in use. Thirdly, a text-based curriculum is resource-based: it offers choices for negotiating the curriculum, for learners' pursuit of individual and group interests, and for the creation and use of local content for inclusion in the curriculum. There is scope for learner autonomy, as well as options for online language learning.

1 Texts in the Fabric of Life

... a great deal of our verbal interaction does involve clearly defined speech events....
We are frequently involved in uses of language in which we only need half a dozen
words, and we can tell immediately what the context of situation is.
Halliday and Hasan (1985: 38)

Introduction

This chapter outlines the centrality of texts in our lives: how texts are
bound up with and constitute meanings for participation in society. We are
born into a web of language use in cultural contexts. We are members of
social groups or communities and together we take part in social practices,
frequently with language. The use of language is vital for our social relationships. The patterned nature of language as texts enables us to participate
socially in speech and writing based on familiarity with people, purposes and
contexts of use. Our socialisation experiences in daily interactions familiar-
ise us with cultural meanings – a lot of the time with language. Language
is one of our significant semiotic systems. In traditional language teaching,
language was extracted from people's experience and reduced to objects
for analysis. Pedagogies were designed to reassemble language objects for
communication. Social theory constructs curricula around learners' familiarity with texts. As language has such a significant role in the mediation of
cultural meanings, texts are central to learning. This is the practical reason
for building a curriculum around the texts of social practices.

Life with Language: The Texts of Social Practices

Texts are integral to everyday life. We organise our lives and those of
others with numerous spoken and written texts – greetings, instructions,
news, emails, telephone calls, calendars, timetables and diaries. Invitations,
weather forecasts, sporting programmes and television shows influence
our decisions, actions and events. We undertake tasks with shopping lists
and in response to letters, emails and SMS messages. We share and reflect

1

Text 1.1 A telephone message

on experiences in Facebook, letters and postcards, in conversations and telephone calls. Texts are so much part of our routines and actions that most of the time we are not aware of using them or of the language which constitutes them: they are threaded into the social fabric of relationships, work and leisure.

Texts embed information about people, places and events. A telephone message records with brevity a great deal of information. My daughter took a telephone call for me yesterday and left the message shown in Text 1.1. The message carries evidence of our family relationships – child, aunty and sister. It shows the informality of my daughter's relationship with me. It contains expectations of action – to telephone the caller. The contextual information in a telephone message – which might include who called, for what purpose and at what time – can enable recognition of the source, context and purpose of the message, and give instructions on what actions to take. The message displays social function and purpose for those familiar with the use of iPhones and social media in society.

When we hear or read a text like this we attempt to interpret the social information in the text. The transcript in Text 1.2 is from a service encounter, an event which involves purchasing something. This service encounter takes place in a theatre before a performance. The interlocutors are a theatre attendant (A) who is selling programmes for a drama performance and a theatre-goer (B) who is considering buying a programme. The theatre-goer enquires about a programme for the performance. As I read the transcript I reconstruct the situation in which it occurs. A theatre attendant offers a theatre-goer assistance, who responds with a question about price. As it is nine dollars the theatre-goer asks to look at the programme first to see if it warrants that much money. The attendant then asks what the theatre-goer

---

A   Hi there, can I help?
B   Um, how much are programmes?
A   They're nine dollars.
B   Oh, right!
      Um, do you mind if I just have a look at it first?
A   No, no, that's fine. Go ahead.
B   Oh, thanks. *[Few moments' pause while B looks at programme]*
A   So, what do you reckon? What's the verdict?
B   Um, yeah, I'll take one thanks.
      Just got to find my money.
      Oh, there you go.
A   Thank you, from twenty, that's 10 and 11 dollars change.
B   Thanks
A   Thank you. See you later.
B   Yeah, seeya.

Text 1.2 Service encounter: Buying a programme at the theatre

has decided. The theatre-goer expresses the wish to purchase it. Payment is made, change is given and greetings are exchanged. Although the transcript displays the interaction out of context, we are able to reconstruct the action from the text. Text, actions, material objects and space are integrated. The transcript illustrates the alignment of language with human activity and physical space. Language use is integral to the actions of making a purchase. Success in spoken interaction results from participants' understanding of what is going on, anticipation of response and prediction of the nature of the response.

We observe, hear and produce texts which convey meanings about contexts, participants and proceedings. We have learned these in our cultural socialisation. From multiple encounters with language we distinguish meanings in language patterns and develop expectations of how language is used for specific purposes. We respond to greetings, answer questions, email responses and read instructions for buying a ticket from a machine. We observe the texts around us – how people talk together, write to each other, read messages and document work. In conversations we monitor minutely the actions and reactions of speakers and fine-tune our language choices for different purposes. Different domains of human activity have different texts. In workplaces we adopt technical language and subject-specific discourses. In relationships we distinguish socially appropriate terms. For participation in events, we observe and draw upon the texts of others. For the expression and composition of our own texts, we seek advice or help from experienced others. Over time we develop discourses appropriate to our roles, to our relationships and to our goals.

Movement from one domain of social activity to another requires learning new texts – learning the specific functions, the local meanings and wordings for the comprehension of, and contribution to, activities. For example, when children go to school they need to learn language for understanding and taking part in school procedures and in defined classroom activities. They experience and learn to produce new texts: texts for participation, for gaining attention and for responding appropriately to instructions. They learn to use the formal discourses of education for school subjects and for specialised topics which have characteristic ways of organising information with maps, diagrams and graphs. Children's and students' engagement in new practices socialises them into uses of appropriate discourses (Mickan, 2006).

Familiarity with texts is essential for relationships, work and leisure. Texts have a direct influence on our behaviours. A weather report in the daily newspaper influences the clothes we wear, the transport we take, the plans we make with family or friends. We change menus, venues and programmes in response to weather forecasts. A shopping list directs movements and interactions in the supermarket or marketplace. A written or voicemail telephone message requires follow-up telephone calls or meetings. Texts enable us to make sense of our experiences and of the experiences of others, such as when we listen to someone retelling an event or read a travel book. The ubiquity, propinquity, utility and significance of texts in our lives make them familiar units for the design of curricula and useful organisers for teaching activities.

Social Practices, Texts and Meanings

Language is a pre-eminent system for making meanings in human culture. It is associated with other systems for making meaning, such as physical gestures, visual representations, material objects, spaces, sounds and movements. Texts are units of meaning. As we grow up we become familiar with meanings of numerous texts. In spoken language we use tone, gestures and volume together with the choice of wordings to vary meanings and to convey nuances of meaning. For written language the signs on the page or screen are of importance in the creation of targeted meanings: the wordings and fonts and layout contribute to the meanings of a text. Language as text is a normal part of sharing meanings with others and making sense of experiences.

Our normal experience of language is to make sense with it. Learning to make meanings is central to a social theory of language. Traditional language education analysed language in linguistic terms as formal grammar not as a system for the expression of meanings. While recent pedagogies such as communicative language teaching and task-based approaches have highlighted communication in language learning, form in terms of grammar, and function in terms of meaning, are treated separately in exercises and explanations. Different conceptions of language underpin traditional language pedagogies and social theory pedagogy. One views language as an object to be described, analysed and studied. The other conceives language as a system for making meanings. Learning to mean is different from learning about rules for language use and the application of grammatical rules out of context. Making meaning with language is not part of doing transformational exercises. Learning language use is not translating lists of sentences or doing grammatical insertion exercises which make no sense.

Encounters with texts evoke specific social meanings. Halliday (1975: 124) points out that 'Text represents the actualization of meaning potential'. Particular word combinations together with page layout and pictures accompanying a text suggest particular meanings. Our normal response to signs and sounds of language is to make sense, to seek meanings. A flyer reproduced in Text 1.3 was put through our letterbox. It deals with a set of culturally related circumstances. When a pet cat or dog goes missing, owners often seek neighbours' help in finding the animal by posting flyers

Text 1.3 Flyer requesting help to find a missing dog

through letterboxes or on fences and trees with information about the loss. In this example, the message is expressed in the wording and visual layout of the text. The text format is printed as a public notice so people recognise its purpose. I construct the dominant meanings in the text as follows:

- **text type** – flyer or poster advertisement to find missing pet dog;
- **culture** – dogs kept as pets;
- **social practice of the text** – find lost animal; appeal to community to assist in locating the pet;
- **topic** – pet dog, as opposed to wild dog;
- **circumstance** – from the perspective of the owners the dog is lost (possibly not the dog's perspective);
- **function of the text** – a request for help to find the dog;
- **relationships** – sympathetic and trustworthy community members who understand owner–dog relationships;
- **mode** – this is a multimodal text, a written notice with a picture of the dog; the notice is circulated in a literate community; it is designed to reach a maximum number of people through duplication and circulation (primarily through people's letterboxes);
- **lexico-grammar** – selection of wording creates meaning potential to achieve social purpose.

When I received the flyer I was able to recognise its function from my past associations with such posters, including the composition of a similar circular when our cat went missing. My understanding of such texts, of the place of dogs in people's lives, of telephones and of messages enables me to recognise what the text is doing and to understand its functions. The offer of a reward tells me the dog is valued. The wordings contain the cultural information for readers to construct the main message of the text: a dog has been lost and the owner of the dog seeks help for its return. These meanings are potentially in the text, but they need to be recreated by readers using their textual experiences, that is, their social experiences with language. When I read the flyer, I viewed the selection and spacing of words as signs conveying meanings. While meanings are encoded in the text, I needed to understand the cultural information within the text in order to make sense of it. The language and the cultural meanings are not separated.

Systemic functional grammar (Halliday, 1994) describes the systematic relationship of language to cultural context:

> the context in which the text unfolds, is encapsulated in the text, not in a kind of piecemeal fashion, not at the other extreme in any mechanical way, but through a systematic relationship between the

social environment on the one hand, and the functional organisation of language on the other. If we treat both text and context as semiotic phenomena, as 'modes of meaning', so to speak, we can get from one to the other in a revealing way. (Halliday & Hasan, 1985: 11–12)

Teaching with texts contextualises culture and embeds social functions, which assists learners to make sense of texts and to recognise the purposes for learning language.

Different Texts for Different Social Practices

In the course of an average day we are involved in many different events with different discourses. So far this morning, I have talked with my wife, read a newspaper, talked with the bus conductor, greeted colleagues, consulted with students, read the text of this chapter and read a dozen emails sent for different purposes – university news and notices, administrative messages, personal notes and students' applications to study here, and I have responded to them. In familiar encounters the language we use is predictable, related to situations and connected to practices, to relationships and to topics. Our choice of wordings varies according to the social purposes and the situations of the actions in which language is embedded. The variations in language range from restricted language selections, in which the choice of words and possible meanings are fixed or very limited, as in road signs, or notices such as 'No Smoking' or 'Exit', to open selections in casual conversations, which might incorporate diverse texts, such as narratives, confessions, reports, appraisals and descriptions.

We vary language selections and patterns according to the purposes and circumstances of speech and composition. We create texts through selections of wordings from a language system. In workplaces we use the technical texts of our work, as well as less formal language connected with informal consultations and activities. For sport, we use terminology for the expression of actions specific to football or tennis or swimming. What we say varies according to our role as coach, player or club supporter. The level of formality of texts is carefully calibrated for interlocutors or readers, according to relationships and purposes. We may be friends with a religious teacher with whom we conduct casual conversations over a meal, but when the teacher preaches to a gathering, a more formal language is spoken. Speakers and writers make choices from grammatical systems of language to carry out different social functions.

Halliday and Hasan (1985: 12) describe a framework for the interpretation of the social context of a text:

1. The Field of Discourse refers to what is happening, to the nature of the social action that is taking place: What is it that the participants are engaged in, in which the language figures as some essential component?
2. The Tenor of Discourse refers to who is taking part, to the nature of the participants, their statuses and roles: ...
3. The Mode of Discourse refers to what part the language is playing, what it is that the participants are expecting the language to do for them in that situation.

Through analysis of language choices in a text, we are able to identify: what the text is about (= the Field); the people involved in the text and their relationships (= the Tenor); and the kind of language in use (= the Mode), such as spoken or written discourses. In texts, Field, Tenor and Mode are in systematic relationships for the realisation of social purposes. The relationships form patterns so that we can speak of text types or genres connected with human practices, such as shopping (service encounters), entertaining (narratives) and informing (reports).

Speakers' and writers' word combinations are based on experiences and expectations of what language selections work to realise specific social functions. The actual lexico-grammatical selections for realising a particular purpose are not predetermined like dialogues written as exercises for memorisation in some language courses. Hasan in Halliday and Hasan (1985) has described optional and obligatory elements which make up texts. With reference to register – a linguistic term distinguishing the contexts and purposes of language events – she explains variations in kinds of register:

> The category of register will vary, from something that is closed and limited to something that is relatively free and open-ended. That is to say, there are certain registers in which the total number of possible meanings is fixed and finite and may be quite small; whereas in others, the range of the discourse is much less constrained. (Halliday & Hasan, 1985: 39)

A text such as EXIT in a public hall has limited meanings. A service encounter has some predictable as well as optional wordings. The obligatory elements are the wordings which constitute the actions of a spoken or written event – those segments of speech which enable the business at hand to take place and to proceed satisfactorily and in a normal and relatively predictable fashion. The optional elements are additional speech items that introduce topics, comments or personal information.

Service encounter	Schematic structure of service encounter
A Hi there, can I help?	Getting attention *
B Um, how much are programmes?	Enquiry *
A They're nine dollars.	Response *
B Oh, right! Um, do you mind if I just have a look at it first?	Enquiry *+
A No, no, that's fine. Go ahead.	Response *
B Oh, thanks. *[Few moments' pause while B looks at programme]*	Response – appreciation +
A So, what do you reckon? What's the verdict?	Question checking if customer wants to purchase +
B Um, yeah, I'll take one thanks. Just got to find my money. Oh, there you go.	Response * Payment +
A Thank you, from 20, that's 10 and 11 dollars change.	Counting out change +
B Thanks.	Greeting – appreciation *
A Thank you. See you later.	Greeting – appreciation * Greeting – farewell +
B Yeah, seeya.	Greeting – response

Text 1.4 Service encounter in a theatre foyer: Obligatory (*) and optional (+) elements

Text 1.4 presents the example of a service encounter referred to previously (Text 1.2) which has obligatory elements (marked with an asterisk, *) as well as optional elements (marked with a plus sign, +). It takes place in the foyer of the theatre shortly before a performance. The elements marked obligatory refer to the main negotiation of the service encounter. It should be noted that the optional elements also have obligations; these, though, are not necessary for this service to be carried out, but rather reflect social obligations and expectations.

We can trace the progression of actions in this service encounter. The minimal obligatory parts for the transaction are indicated. It is noticeable that very little language is required for the activity of purchasing a programme. In fact, the purchase of the programme could have taken place without the attendant or theatre-goer speaking at all. As is often the case, the transaction is accompanied by other verbal requests and responses. The

Service encounter	Obligatory and optional elements
A How are you today?	Obligatory although optional in today's supermarket exchanges
B Not bad thanks? How are you?	Obligatory
A I'm good thank you. Did you want this in a bag?	Obligatory Optional
B No, it's fine by itself.	Optional
A That's 35 dollars and 25 cents. Do you have Fly Buys [the customer loyalty scheme]?	Obligatory Optional
B No. I'll put that on my debit card.	Optional
A Did you want any cash out?	Optional
B No, thank you.	Optional
A PIN number and 'Okay'. Here's your receipt. Have a good day.	Optional but depends on context Optional Obligatory
B Thank you. You too.	Obligatory Optional

Text 1.5 Service encounter in a supermarket with optional and obligatory turns

exchange shows a sequence in the spoken turns – the schematic structure and the alignment of physical with verbal actions. The language selections are specific to this particular encounter, but also have evidence of a more general social practice, a service encounter involving the exchange of goods, as in Text 1.5. This service encounter takes place in a supermarket in Adelaide, South Australia. As with the previous encounter, the actual transaction could have taken place without speaking, which is almost normal for a large supermarket. When we read the transcript, we reconstruct the material actions in the supermarket: the attendant preparing to place the items in a plastic bag after she has recorded the price; taking out the credit card; inserting the credit card into the automatic transmission device and pressing buttons to transmit the electronic information necessary for paying for the shopping. We reconstruct the progression of the actions from the text. The schematic structure of the spoken words is created as a sequence in conjunction with the actions.

For those familiar with supermarkets and checkout attendants, the words evoke images of the situation and of participants' actions. This is clearly not, say, a farmers' market where the purchase of items is by negotiation with individuals and where buyers can bargain with sellers. The text reveals details of the situation and the culture to those familiar with the particular actions of purchasing in supermarkets. The actions and the language or texts go hand-in-hand. The verbal exchange would be different in a small, local shop where customer and proprietor know and therefore greet each other and where the proprietor picks out items requested by the purchaser. There we would ask for an item, make reference to the exchange of monies ('How much is it?') as the obligatory elements and, if we had time, we could talk about people or shared topics as optional elements. In such instances, the actual social purpose of the event, that is, the exchange of goods, is connected with the maintenance of relationships. Certain obligatory phrases may remain, such as greetings, requests for items and payment details, but other elements could vary. The participants in normal language encounters utilise their familiarity with social customs in a location for the moment-by-moment selection of wordings for the construction of texts.

Speech events, both oral and written, show how the physical and linguistic actions in social encounters are structured and patterned. People's actions in contexts – their social practices – structure the patterns of talk and take place through the talk. The inseparability of the linguistic pattern from participants' actions is apparent in the sequence of actions unfolding with the linguistic activity. The connections of language to human action and to the predictability and repetitiveness of patterned human behaviour make possible the analysis of text types or genres. The interrelationship of human action with text types forms the organisational basis for designing curricula around social practices.

Texts and the Curriculum

Texts are cultural artefacts. When we see and hear texts we attempt to make sense of them, to understand them. We situate texts with practices to make sense of the meanings. Our response to language we hear or read is to make sense of it, which is why we say to incomprehensible language 'It doesn't make sense!' Students in language lessons experience frustration with repeated questions such as 'What is your name?', 'What colour is this?', to which a teacher already knows the answer – these are irrational language exchanges which trivialise language use. In such exchanges speakers are not expressing meanings. Such exchanges are radically different from students' out-of-class conversations, where they use language with purpose in their relationships, in order to get things done, in joint action and to influence people.

The human experience of seeking to find and to make meanings with systems of signs is the foundation of a social practices curriculum. Meaning making is what we do continually, very often with language, and in instructional contexts a great deal with language. Our first reaction to texts, to spoken and written phenomena in our environment, is to make sense of them, to understand them. Encounters with texts have meaning potential – the potential for people to create socially shared personal and public meanings. The potential enables different meanings to be made as each encounter with texts offers new opportunities to make sense of them. A curriculum constructed around social practices and their texts is a curriculum designed for learners' engagement with meaning – not as an afterthought, but as the central activity. The focus on texts creates potential to make meanings with other people.

Summary

Texts are part of our everyday experiences of meaning-making. We use language in our daily practices with intricate connections between our actions and speech, between context and language use, between physical environment and human activity. The alignment of language and actions reflects expectations and predictions about patterns of language appropriate to particular occasions. We recognise texts by their patterns. Varieties of language, or text types, arise from varieties of social practice. When we compose texts we select wordings to create these patterns. We can describe the patterns if we stop to reflect on what was said, as we often do in recounting conversations at dinner parties, at work or in the company of friends. It is the patterned nature of texts calibrated for the realisation of social practices which enables the identification of text types for teaching language. Text types focus attention on similarities of language use associated with similar social practices.

Notes and Readings

The study of meaning is an important topic in linguistics. Various perspectives on it can be studied in the areas of semiotics, semantics and pragmatics, which to some extent developed as sub-disciplines of linguistics to compensate for the inadequacies of structural descriptions of language. An influential paper by Malinowski (1994) provides an historical backdrop for later work in semiotics. Hodge and Kress (1988) give an account of the situated nature of signs and messages in social relations and processes.

Halliday's (1978) book *Language as Social Semiotic: The Social Interpretation of Language and Meaning* is a seminal work for this chapter. Halliday's (2004) *An Introduction to Functional Grammar* has been most influential. A survey of Halliday's papers on systemic functional linguistics has been recently published (Webster, 2003–2009; see also Webster, 2009). Halliday (1975: 123) identified the essential properties of text as meaning and choice. According to Halliday (1975: 124), a text is a unit of meaning which is encoded in wordings selected from options in the language system: 'a text is a semantic structure that is formed out of a continuous process of choice among innumerable interrelated sets of semantic options'. When we use language we draw upon the meaning potential in the language system to create meanings specific to our purposes at the time. A collection of essays written by Hasan and edited by Cloran *et al.* (1996) gives a rich account of text and context and realisation of meanings with language.

I have used the terms 'text' and 'text types' in this chapter and elsewhere in preference to 'genre', but much of what is outlined in this chapter is written about elsewhere from the perspective of genre pedagogy. The essays in Cope and Kalantzis (1993) introduce genre pedagogy. Butt *et al.* (2000) apply systemic functional grammar to teaching genres. A somewhat different perspective can be gained from Gee's (1990) book on discourses. Publications by Martin and Rose (2005, 2008) contain systematic approaches to the analysis of texts.

Ventola's (1987) analysis of service encounters is an account of the language of a particular kind of social practice – obtaining services. She studied the interactions in service encounters, looking at how spoken interactions are organised through patterned, linguistic choices. She wrote: 'Social encounters are systems where social processes, which realize the social activity, unfold in stages and, in doing so, achieve a certain goal or purpose' (Ventola, 1987: 1). The main structural elements of service encounters according to Ventola (1987) are: *Greeting – getting attention → Request for goods → Response → Goods delivered → Payment → Parting – appreciation shown.* The social practice of making a face-to-face purchase and the structure of the discourse are aligned.

What is interesting in the case of service encounters is how the discourse changes with technological change. Supermarkets have introduced self-service so that customers can scan in the barcodes of items and scan credit cards to pay for them. The electronic purchase of groceries has introduced new social practices, so that customers need to read different literacy and numeracy texts (barcodes, electronic instructions, credit cards) which do not require speaking but depend on physical manipulation of keys and entry of data.

Tasks

(1) Record and transcribe a speech event. Analyse the language of the text and identify the actual wordings which suggest to you the place, time, purpose and people involved in the speech event. What is going on¿ Where does the transcribed spoken interaction take place¿ Who is involved¿ What is being transacted¿

(2) Each day, we use and encounter many texts. Using a notebook or electronic device, attempt to record the texts you experience, either observed or used, in the course of a day. An analysis of the texts could begin with simply noting them as spoken or written; then go deeper in the analysis and specify the social purpose of the language and still further the different selections of grammar and vocabulary (the lexico-grammar) which differentiate the texts and realise the social functions.

(3) Observe a lesson, either teaching an additional language or teaching one of the subjects in the curriculum. Write down as far as possible the variety of oral and written texts used during the lesson, starting with the teacher's lesson introduction. Record the spoken and written texts and note some of the differences in the wordings of the texts for doing different things in class.

(4) Record with an audio- or video-recorder your language use in a speech event, such as asking for some food, reporting an experience, giving someone instructions. Transcribe the recording. What is the pattern of language use¿ Explain your choice of words: what influenced your selection of wordings¿

(5) In our workplaces many of us use a lot of language. Document the language of a workplace for one day or, to begin with, for part of a day, recording spoken and written varieties and the different purposes for which language is used.

(6) In relation to a transcript you have recorded, comment on the following quote from Hasan and Williams (1996: xi): 'Texts are by definition socially situated acts of semiosis, and therefore necessarily variable as a function of their relation to the social context of use, which both defines and is defined by them'.

2 Change and Renewal in Curriculum Design

The important thing about the nature of a text is that, although when we write it down it looks as though it is made of words and sentences, it is really made of meanings.
Halliday and Hasan (1985: 10)

Introduction

The reason for proposing a curriculum design based on social theory is outlined in this chapter. Curriculum renewal is needed in response to sociocultural conceptions of language in use and in particular in response to our understanding of language as a social semiotic.

Changes in Curriculum Design

The language curriculum has changed a lot since I studied Ancient Greek, German and Latin in school. Some of the section headings listed in the contents page of the Latin textbook which I studied in school (Kennedy, 1959) are shown in Text 2.1. The section topics show that the unit of analysis was grammatical, beginning with the alphabet and progressing to more complex items of syntax. Learning Latin meant learning grammatical rules of written

Section		Page
1	The Latin Language	1
2	The Alphabet	2
3	Vowels and Consonants	2
8a	Syllables	5
10	Sound Changes	6
24	Inflexion	11
25	Parts of Speech	12
28	Declension and Gender	13

Text 2.1 Contents page of a Latin textbook

15

language independently of language use. Discourse features essential for speaking or writing Latin were introduced late in the teaching programme: in section 181A, page 113 of the Latin textbook, the syntax of the sentence was introduced. Sentences were analysed as isolated structural units. The study of Latin was a linguistic activity. Most lesson time was spent writing and reciting written exercises, with the teacher correcting errors.

I also studied Ancient Greek and German, for which the grammatical focus was the same as for Latin. Admittedly in German we studied different topics but these were written in order to introduce grammatical items. The first four chapters of a German textbook had the following headings (Orton, 1968: 7):

Chapter 1.   **Die Familie**. The definite article
Chapter 2.   **Peter und Maria**. The indefinite article
Chapter 3.   **Der Onkel ist hier**. The verb sein. Formation of questions and negatives
Chapter 4.   **Tanzmusik.** The regular verb spielen

The chapters mix topical themes with grammar items 'illustrating essential points of grammar' (Orton, 1968: 5). There was no principled or logical relationship between topics and grammar. Texts were written to teach grammar, not to inform or entertain. These contrived texts were unrelated to social purposes. The German language was represented as an abstract structural system, and learning German as a process of acquiring knowledge about the language system. Teachers and lecturers used the textbooks as substitutes for a curriculum. Official syllabus documents listed grammatical items to be taught in a year level. The grammar list corresponded to the content of the textbook. Texts about the family and Peter and Maria were fictional. The study of German lacked authenticity and topics were irrelevant for students interested in the lives of Germans and in communicating in German.

In the 1960s the language curriculum needed to change. The mobility of workers and travellers created a demand to learn local languages for working and travelling in different countries. Language policies extended language education to all children, including the introduction of language programmes in primary schools. The subsequent changes to curricula and pedagogy are traced in Table 2.1, which summarises influential approaches to syllabus and curriculum design over the last 50 years. Although the different designs have been labelled as distinctive, in practice a new curriculum was often an amalgam of elements from previous designs. Table 2.1 highlights selected characteristics of the different designs. The analysis of change

Table 2.1 Summary of changes in curriculum designs during the last 50 years

Curriculum design	Theoretical perspective	Units of analysis	Students' main activities	Comments
Grammar translation	Structural linguistics; descriptions of parts of sentences; learning rules of language	Inventory of grammatical structures; lists of vocabulary items	Memorise words and rules; write exercises and translate sentences; study simplified written passages which illustrate grammar and vocabulary	Emphasis on language as form not for use; focus on written language; advanced learners read and analyse original novels, plays, poetry
Situational curriculum	Stereotypical dialogues associated with specified speech situations	Contrived, written dialogues; traditional grammar	Learn written dialogues by rote; act out role-plays	Predetermined and artificial speech; fixed relationship between situations and dialogues
Audio-lingual audio-visual	Behaviourism: theory = learn through imitation	Pre-scripted, written dialogues recorded on tape with accompanying slide pictures	Listen to and repeat dialogues; imitation of set dialogues; practise variations	Repetition of artificial dialogues and invented contexts
Functional-notional curriculum	Speech act theory	Functions: to agree to request to refuse. Notions: time, place	Practise speech acts in simulated activities	Language-centred; decontextualised speech acts
Communicative language teaching	Learn language through spoken interaction	Information exchange; includes elements from other models	Language activities such as information gap tasks	Oral emphasis; rehearsal for authentic language use out of class
Task-based curriculum	Negotiation of meaning through doing tasks	Tasks and grammar of tasks	Interactive tasks for negotiation of meaning	Language of tasks indeterminate
Content-based curriculum (bilingual and immersion programmes)	Learn language through study of subject content	Course content: experiments in science, topics in history	Tasks and texts associated with subject learning (e.g. science experiments)	Use of target language for authentic purposes
Genre-based curriculum	Texts as social semiotic products and processes	Text types or genres – oral and written	Genre analysis and composition; written focus	Focus on lexico-grammar of genre
Text-based curriculum	Language as social semiotic	Oral and written texts constitute and constituted by social practices	Realisation of social purposes via text-based spoken and written activities and text analysis	Language use and analysis integrated with social practices

summarised in Table 2.1 demonstrates repeated attempts to reconstitute decontextualised grammar into texts for communication with additions of speech acts, functions and notions, situational dialogues, communicative activities, tasks and genres.

Grammar translation

In traditional language education, the study of languages was exclusively for students who were selected on the results of language aptitude tests. Languages study was academically difficult, for a select few with sufficient skill to read and analyse literature. The curriculum was economical and sparse, simply listing grammatical forms as core content, usually set out in textbooks and reading books. Teaching was essentially about explaining rules of grammar, which were illustrated with artificial texts. Students applied grammar rules in meaningless written exercises and translations for correction by a teacher. Corrections were normally done in class, which, apart from grammatical explanations, was the usual interaction between teachers and students. Normally teachers did not use the target language for grammatical instruction. Oral language was practised only to develop accurate pronunciation for reading words or sentences aloud.

The persistent problem with grammar teaching was the need for students to reconstitute grammatical components or parts of language for communication. This took a long time, during which the enthusiasm of students for learning the language dissipated because most of them did not experience any progress in using language in ways familiar to them in their first languages. A second problem was that grammatical knowledge did not translate into language use nor transfer to different communicative functions. The structural description of grammar was disconnected from social contexts and functions of language in use. A small number of advanced students after years of study had positive experiences reading and analysing original texts – novels, plays, poems and short stories. The experience of extensive reading and literary analysis of original texts for meaning explained the success of the few students who achieved some degree of fluency under this teaching method.

Situational curriculum

The main aim of the situational curriculum was the development of students' spoken skills for participation in defined communicative events. The content of the curriculum consisted of dialogues assumed to be typical of spoken transactions in situations such as at the post office, in the bank or at the butcher. The dialogues were contrived and written formally. Students read and repeated dialogues in order to memorise them. Traditional grammar continued to be taught, but it was a grammar of written language, not of actual speech.

The situational curriculum responded to students' desire and need to learn to speak a language. A major problem, however, was the artificial nature of the written dialogues, which did not resemble the highly interactive nature of spoken language. The rote learning of dialogues was boring, with students reciting artificial phrases like parrots. The usefulness of dialogues was limited for actual face-to-face communication for different purposes.

Audio-visual/audio-lingual curriculum

The audio-visual or audio-lingual curriculum introduced technology to language teaching in the form of tape-recorders and slide presentations installed in high-tech, interactive language laboratories. Recordings of spoken language enabled learners to listen to and repeat native speakers' pronunciation. Students wearing headphones sat in separate booths and listened to and repeated recorded dialogues in order to produce accurate pronunciation. The learning theory conceived language learning in terms of habit formation – the internalisation of expressions through lots of repetition. Similar to the situational curriculum, students repeated dialogues which in audio-visual courses had accompanying, static slides depicting speakers' exchanges in sequence. The artificial, memorised dialogues did not prepare students for joining in classroom communication, let alone conversation.

The installation of dedicated laboratories for language study at first conferred technical prestige on the subject, but students became bored with repeating pre-recorded drills while sitting in booths separated from other students. The isolation and impersonal interactions with a teacher through microphones alienated students. Once the novelty of the technology wore off, students began to damage and deface equipment and furniture. Abandoned language laboratories bear witness to the significant failure of audio-lingual teaching.

Functional-notional curriculum

In the functional-notional curriculum the units of analysis were speech acts. The speech acts or functions were listed as learning objectives – to invite, to refuse, to like. Time, place and manner were listed as separate items or notions. The curriculum was structured around concepts which were readily adaptable to teaching: expressing likes and dislikes, inviting, refusing. The curriculum included topics selected for their relevance to students' experiences and to future plans for travel and work. Students rehearsed refusing, inviting, expressing likes and dislikes with classmates.

The functional-notional curriculum was a breath of fresh air in languages teaching because students interacted using speech acts. Attention was on the way people actually spoke rather than on the routine reproduction of complete sentences. However, the language functions were based on linguistic analysis which connected selected lexico-grammar to the performance of particular speech acts. The problem is that a so-called 'function' – a request or a refusal or an invitation – can be realised linguistically in a variety of ways. The tying of speech acts to specific linguistic exponents constrained speech, limiting students' abilities to make meanings in a target language.

Communicative language teaching

Communicative language teaching, although introduced over 30 years ago, continues to influence educational policies, programmes and practices. The goal of communication prioritises authentic, spoken language. It assumes a theory of learning to make meanings through authentic language use. In practice, communicative language teaching is more complex. The approach refocused the curriculum on communication without discarding elements from previous models: to traditional grammar as a core component of instruction it added functions and notions, activity types, learning strategies and discourse features. The additional elements made the curriculum unwieldy, increasing the time needed for teachers' lesson preparation and requiring skilled class management. But the focus on authentic language and communicative activities rejuvenated teaching in some contexts, particularly where classes were relatively small, teachers' proficiency was high, and where colourful, multimodal resources were available, and classroom conditions were conducive to oral work in pairs and groups.

Communicative methodology has drawbacks and has not been implemented satisfactorily in many contexts. The first drawback is a conflicted learning theory which claims learning through making meaning, but teaches traditional grammar and grammatical exercises. The second is an overloaded pedagogy, with traditional sentence-level description of grammar and exercises, plus notions and functions, plus communicative strategies, plus contrived activities. A third is an assumption that classrooms are not good places to learn to communicate, so that so-called authentic out-of-class discourses – learner as foreign traveller – were introduced at the expense of communication in class communities. The drawbacks have consequences: a dominance of teachers' questioning, repetitive speech exchanges, irrelevant choice of topics and disillusioned learners. The communicative curriculum has been resilient and it has incorporated new elements as insights into the nature of communication have changed; but it has not dealt with a misconception of language as the object of instruction. The model has failed to reconceptualise language as social semiotic.

Task-based curriculum

In a task-based model the curriculum is structured around tasks which require language use, for example for problem-solving, for the exchange of opinions and for decision-making. Underpinned by a learning theory which explains second-language acquisition in terms of the negotiation of meanings, learners take part in tasks using a target language. When learners do not understand a speaker, they seek explanation or repetition or rephrasing, that is, they negotiate meanings. Tasks are structured so that learners are required to use selected syntactic items. The attention to selected target language items in this process stimulates cognitive processing, leading to internalisation of new grammatical elements and reorganisation of learners' inter-language. The positive advantages of task-based teaching are an articulated learning theory, learners' use of language for carrying out tasks with tangible outcomes, language integrated in the text-based activities and grammar analysed as a construct of particular tasks.

Implementation of a task-based curriculum requires teachers with advanced proficiency, readily available resources for participation in tasks, and classroom conditions conducive to students working together in a target language. Without these conditions the implementation of a task-based curriculum is daunting. Apart from the external conditions needed for teaching through tasks, there are more fundamental problems. One is that tasks can be performed with different selections of lexico-grammar so that the pre-determination of the selected language items for performing tasks is difficult. It is also possible for students to complete tasks without use of the target language. At a more fundamental level the model continues a tradition of measurement of language development in terms of grammatical structures.

Content-based curriculum

Another curriculum model is the teaching of content subjects in a target language. Bilingual programmes and immersion programmes are well known examples. The goal of content programmes is learning the content of subjects, such as science, or art or history. In bilingual programmes language is integrated with subject-defining activities. Teachers and students use the target language to work together.

Despite the success of content-based pedagogies, organisational factors have contributed to limited implementation of content teaching: teachers need high proficiency in the target language and also qualifications as subject-specific specialists; appropriate resources are required to teach subject content; and administrators face structural difficulties with time-tabling and sequencing classes of bilingual learners across levels of schooling. Such practical difficulties have restricted the implementation of content pro-grammes, except in countries such as Canada, where immersion programmes have been institutionally integrated into education systems.

Genre-based curriculum

The aim of a genre curriculum is to develop students' skills in analysis of the purposes and wordings of different texts and in composing texts. Genre pedagogy was initially based on the analysis and classification of written texts. Underpinned by systemic functional grammar (Halliday, 1994), language is recognised as a resource for making meanings in sociocultural contexts. Meanings in texts are realised through generic structure and the selection of words and grammar (lexico-grammar) specific to social functions and cultural contexts. Certain patterns or constellations of language choices in texts make up genres – the reasonably predictable wordings for text types such as argument essays, scientific reports or narratives. Complete and authentic texts are the units of analysis and focus of classroom activities. Learners study the textual organisation and structural patterns which characterise the functions of texts. They are taught a metalanguage for the identification of wordings which constitute different genres and the language system. Learners accumulate textual resources and know-how for composing their own texts.

Genre teaching has been criticised for teaching genres as predictable and normative social discourses, to which students need to conform. The advantage for students is that working with whole texts and with the focus on language as a resource for the expression of meanings, they learn to analyse lexico-grammatical selections. They are able to recognise wording differences between genres and to apply the analysis to their compositions.

Text-based curriculum

Texts are embedded in social practices so the curriculum focuses attention on people's purposes for language use. Texts are both oral and written. Text and genre designs are very similar, but with the distinction that the social purpose of texts are foregrounded in the former. The priority is to determine what is going on in a context and how language is integral to what is taking place. The design is elaborated in the following chapters.

Curriculum Renewal

The review above illustrates curriculum designers' attempts to compensate for the extraction of language from context in traditional language education by adding new elements to the components of grammar and vocabulary. In languages education we have become accustomed to working with dismantled language objects, which need to be reassembled. Second-language learning theories and methodologies have been constructed around grammatical components of language, extracted from context and dissected into parts of syntax, lexis and phonology, which no longer function to make social meanings. The dissection of language is evident in prevalent dichotomies and distinctions: between form and function, language and culture, syntax and lexis, simple and complex, language use and language exercises, authentic and artificial discourses, cognitive and social elements. In consequence, languages pedagogy has had to use dismantled items of language to reconstruct texts and purposes for language use. The review shows up a kind of plastic surgery, with curriculum changes revealing attempts to rehabilitate emaciated and mechanical conceptions of communication.

Curriculum designers have attempted the reconstitution and recontextualisation of language in an approximation of communicative events by adding pragmatic, cultural and situational elements to grammar and lexis. This has been an attempt to reintegrate language into contexts from which it had been separated in the first place. The problem with patching up communication in this way is that the original grammar template has not been re-analysed but has been retained and supplemented with new elements – functions and notions, speech acts for negotiation of meanings, learning strategies and task typologies.

Unresolved Issues in Curriculum Models

The changes in curricula mapped out above have not culminated in a model which is compact, practical and adaptable to the different conditions under which languages are taught. Problems of implementation, teacher preparation, grammatical testing and poor learning outcomes persist. The almost continual search for an improved curriculum in response to new programme goals, changing learner profiles and new technologies is evidence of the inadequacies of the preceding models, but also of the energy and commitment of teachers and researchers to the improvement of language instruction. But each change has added to the complexity of the curriculum, without a re-examination of the theoretical foundations of the designs.

A survey of curriculum designs exposes a pattern in the changes. There are three significant trends.

(1) There has been a continuing re-appraisal of what it is to teach a language, and in that process there has been a reluctance to give up previous conceptions of language. This is exhibited in the retention of grammar as a measure of language acquisition.
(2) In order to compensate for shortcomings in the description of language in structural terms, the models have added elements to the curriculum in a cumulative process. To syntax and lexis have been added copious elements, in particular functions and notions, learners' roles and identities, communicative activities and tasks, composing strategies and learning strategies, and discourse features of texts.
(3) The unit of analysis has expanded from discrete and abstract linguistic items to pedagogical tasks and communicative activities.

Despite changes in design, the review above suggests unresolved issues, which continue to confront curriculum planners today. The issues include:

- persistence of grammatical orientation which distinguishes form from function;
- second-language acquisition analysed in terms of the accumulation of syntactical and lexical items;
- dominance of a speaker–receiver or transmitter model of communication in the input–interaction–output/uptake exchange;
- pedagogy of transmission of knowledge about language and its uses;
- analysis of language decontextualised from the intricate, interwoven use of language involved in human transactions;
- language analysed as an object rather than as a social semiotic.

In the next section I will consider these issues.

Dichotomies in Curriculum Design

A curriculum in its simplest form is an inventory of what is to be taught, and how it will be taught and assessed for the realisation of particular goals or specific needs. It is primarily a selection of content, resources and activities organised and sequenced for consistency and continuity of instruction, and for the assessment of change or development. Selecting the content in traditional language teaching was seemingly easy. Grammar items were sequenced from simple to more complex, as with simple sentences to sentences with embedded clauses, or with the present tense of verbs to irregular and conditional verb forms. Analysis of speech and literacy events has made the task of selection more difficult, given descriptions of language variations with complex syntax and discourse organisation.

The central problem for curriculum designers persists – analysis of language as separate from social practices, that is, from contexts of use. Language examined out of context is distinctly different from the way we work with language in daily life. The separation of language from context underpins the dichotomies in language education of form and function, language and culture, grammar and meaning, and the listing as discrete skills of speaking, listening, reading and writing. The consistent feature of the dichotomies is the treatment of language as separate from context, or more specifically from the social practices integral to language use. The nature of the dichotomies is discussed in the sections below.

Form and function

Language teaching has been pre-occupied with the surface features of language at the sentence level. It has disconnected discourses from contexts of use. The separation of form from function, grammar from language use, is deeply ingrained in language pedagogy. There is an assumption that language development equates to the accumulation of grammatical items and words. There is also the persistent belief that it is necessary to learn knowledge of language forms prior to making meanings or participating in communication. This view is underscored by the measurement of language development as the acquisition of syntactical elements or lexical items, whether in terms of T-units or length of sentences, clause complexity or lexical range. The acquisition of discrete grammatical elements of a language is taken as an indicator of language development. The basic notion is that the development of learners' internalised grammar results from conscious attention to grammatical forms. The restructuring necessary for extending learners' inter-language requires the learning of forms or structures as identifiable and distinctive elements. The measure of development is grammatical. Communicative and task-based approaches have continued the separate treatment of form and function. Communicative syllabuses recommend a focus on meaning in conjunction with attention to form. The reconciliation of form and function in task-based teaching is only partially accomplished by lining up selected grammatical exponents related to the conduct of particular tasks.

A second problem is that language is treated usually at the sentence level and not at the level of text, that is, not as discourse. Components of sentences are insufficient units of analysis for language teaching when the instructional objective is to develop learners' communicative skills. Structural items of grammar cannot be used as resources for expression of meaning. This is most obviously illustrated in transformation exercises, in which students change verb tenses, or pronouns or persons in separate sentences regardless of purpose or participants. The exercises are often unrelated sentences. Such work focuses on the identification of component parts without analysis of the items as meaning-making elements. Language, in other words, is divorced from its social functions and meanings associated with language in use. Lexical and syntactic items are studied in isolation from the functions they serve in social practices. The semiotic functions of language in society are disregarded. Language is not viewed as a system from which choices are made to express particular meanings. As a result, the way the grammar works as a meaning-making resource is not evident.

Language and culture

Another persistent dichotomy in language education is the distinction between language and culture. It is not unusual for the language curriculum to have separate cultural and linguistic goals and strands. The dismantling of language into grammar and vocabulary as form and function displaces culture. It often leads to stereotypical cultural representations of peoples, places and ways of living. The disjunction of language from culture necessitates the injection of culture back into teaching activities and content. But language is a cultural artefact and language use is embedded in cultural practices. The meanings we make with language are culturally constituted. The lost-dog flyer (Text 1.3) is an example of cultural expression. We recognise the meanings of linguistic signs because of our cultural knowledge of the operation of signs in society. The separation of language from culture in instruction reduces the potential for expression of meanings.

Skills and strategies

Language reductionism extends to the common practice of dividing language use into separate skills. We teach and test skills discretely. In some cases, skills are broken down further, for example teaching reading begins with phonics and study of letters of the alphabet, quite apart from meanings in texts. The separate listing of skills is part of the segregation of language from social use. As I write this text, I am also reading it and I am actually saying it too. Speech involves voicing and listening. The integration of so-called language skills is normal in human interaction.

Cognitive theories of learning have identified learning strategies and learning styles. The identification of strategies and learning processes dissociate meaning-making from communicative events. Processes are categorised as abstractions separate from semiotic function in texts. Instruction in learning and communication strategies extends the dissection of language use into discrete objects. The separate treatment of strategies and processes is another instance of dismantling language from people's practices.

Classroom language use

Classrooms have gained the reputation for being poor environments for authentic communication. The response has been to plan curricula and design textbooks with contrived situations in which students have to imagine they are tourists or foreign citizens and take on pretend names and roles. Such pretences are further instances of students' encounters with unreal and meaningless language. The scenarios they are expected to act out – at a restaurant, being an exchange student – are often beyond their experiences and understanding. The attempt to authenticate communication with such scenarios has had the opposite effect, resulting in artificial dialogues, fake texts and phoney, insincere verbal exchanges between teachers and students.

The injection of so-called out-of-class, authentic language misinterprets the social situation of lessons and of the situated nature of discourse. Such contrivances do not recognise normal language practices in lessons and do not utilise the authenticity of institutional discourses. In fact, classrooms are social environments designed for communicative language use and thus for language learning. We observe this in other areas of the curriculum, where language has not been separated as content from practices. Classroom documentation shows teachers and students work extensively with authentic discourses for the conduct of content-specific tasks – just as we do outside of the classroom.

Summary

The direction of changes in curriculum design for teaching languages since the late 1960s has been from the analysis of discrete and abstract linguistic items, as in grammar/translation methodology, to contextualised, holistic units of analysis, as in communicative and task-based curricula. Different curriculum models have attempted to deal with basic dichotomies of form and function, language and culture, by adding in speech acts, situations, authentic documents and tasks. Curriculum designers face an array of disparate features of language derived from varying theories of language and learning. Traditional analysis with the separation of language from social practices helps to explain the great difficulty teachers and curriculum planners have had reconstituting language for instruction, so that students experience and learn the meaning potential of language use. Curriculum writers have had to deal with dichotomies by recontextualising language segments, and by reintegrating them into tasks and activities. The piecemeal approach to fixing language for communication has resulted in a potpourri of disparate elements, which even in the mended or repaired state do not resemble language in action. For this reason, a curriculum with a coherent and integrated design is needed.

Curriculum designs represent choices from a large range of possible options for structuring programmes, for choosing materials, for teaching and testing. The dismemberment of language from social practices is not necessary. In Chapter 3 I consider how learning takes place through participation in social practices, through processes of socialisation and of apprenticeship. The choice of texts as units of analysis for the curriculum reflects a change in language education, away from the analysis of discrete, decontextualised elements of language, to units of meaning, to social discourse in contexts of use.

Notes and Readings

We generally do not take time to review developments which have led to our current teaching approaches, but the changes in curriculum design and curriculum theory make interesting reading. I suggest that at some time you select and review books influential in the development of current designs for a curriculum. For those interested in checking out some of the claims made about teaching methodologies and curriculum designs in this chapter, I have listed some reference books.

Functions and notions

- Finocchiaro and Brumfit (1983), *The Functional-Notional Approach: From Theory to Practice*;
- Van Ek (1977), *The Threshold Level for Modern Language Learning in Schools*;
- Wilkins (1976), *Notional Syllabuses*.

Communicative language teaching

- Johnson (1982), *Communicative Syllabus Design and Methodology*;
- Littlewood (1981), *Communicative Language Teaching*;
- Munby (1978), *Communicative Syllabus Design*;
- Widdowson (1978), *Teaching Language as Communication*;
- Yalden (1983), *The Communicative Syllabus: Evolution, Design and Imple-mentation*.

Task-based curriculum

- Crookes and Gass (1993a), *Tasks in a Pedagogical Context*;
- Crookes and Gass (1993b), *Tasks and Language Learning*;
- Nunan (1989), *Designing Tasks for the Communicative Classroom*;
- Van Lier (1996), *Interaction in the Language Curriculum*.

Content-based curriculum

- Baker (1993), *Foundations of Bilingual Education and Bilingualism*;
- De Zarobe and Catalan (2009), *Content and Language Integrated Learning*.

Genre theory

- Christie and Martin (2000), *Genre and Institutions*;
- Cope and Kalantzis (1993), *The Powers of Literacy*;
- Hyland (2004b), *Genre and Second Language Writing*;
- Martin and Rose (2005), *Working with Discourse*;
- Martin and Rose (2008), *Genre Relations*;
- Paltridge (2001), *Genre and the Language Learning Classroom*.

Two books by David Nunan (1988a, 1988b) give excellent overviews of different designs for syllabuses and curricula. A recent detailed survey of curriculum design has been written by Nation and Macalister (2010).

I have reviewed teaching approaches over the past 40 years in a book chapter (Mickan, 2004) which analyses teaching approaches from a social perspective.

Numerous studies have looked at the issues raised in this chapter, not necessarily from a curriculum perspective, but which help us to understand the problems I have described. The broader issues which underpin curriculum design can be viewed from an anthropological perspective. Duranti and Goodwin (1995), *Rethinking Context*, is particularly recommended.

The study of discourse has been particularly influential.

- McCarthy (1991), *Discourse Analysis for Language Teachers*;
- McCarthy and Carter (1994), *Language as Discourse*;
- Paltridge (2006), *Discourse Analysis*.

Researchers are giving increasing attention to social theories of learning:

- Kramsch (2002), *Language Acquisition and Language Socialization*;
- Lantolf (2000), *Sociocultural Theory and Second Language Learning*.

Tasks

(1) Discuss or debate with your friends the following statements. With which statements do you agree/disagree?
- A knowledge of grammar is necessary for authentic communication.
- Vocabulary is the fundamental building block of a language.
- Beginning learners cannot communicate in the target language in their first lessons.
- We construct grammar from simple forms to complex.
- Doing grammatical exercises is necessary to internalise rules of language usage. You can take the language out of the culture but you can't take the culture out of the language.

(2) Select a language teaching textbook or teaching programme or syllabus. Study the contents in order to identify its characteristic features. To which curriculum design in Table 2.1 would you assign it? Does it exemplify some of the problems outlined in this chapter?

(3) If you are teaching or have access to a teaching programme for observation, undertake an analysis of its features of the programme. For the analysis, consider the following questions: Is there separation of form from function? Are language and culture treated separately? Is the description of language at the level of the sentence or the text?

(4) Analyse your own teaching programme. How would you describe it in terms of curriculum design? What features of the curriculum (content, activities) mark the curriculum as a particular type? You might use the framework introduced in Table 2.1 to determine the main features.

Curriculum design	Theoretical perspective	Units of analysis	Students' main activities	Comments

(5) Texts are cultural artefacts. They embed cultural information. Select a text and discuss what cultural information is embedded in the text. What wording in the text alerts you to the cultural information?

3 Learning the Language of Social Practices

Learning is, above all, a social process:… Knowledge is transmitted in social context, through relationships, like those of parent and child, or teacher and pupil, or classmates, that are defined in the value systems and ideology of the culture. And the words that are exchanged in these contexts get their meaning from activities in which they are embedded, which again are social activities with social agencies and goals.
Halliday and Hasan (1985: 5)

Introduction

This chapter describes a social theory of language learning. Learning community participation with language is a complex process of socialisation. The argument is that we live in relationships and learn through relationships. By taking part in the practices of communities we learn to understand and use semiotic resources for building and maintaining relationships with other members, and for contributing to the development of knowledge and skills. The purpose of education is the planned preparation of learners for living and working in communities with specialised practices. Shared values, activities, aspirations and accumulated knowledge of how to do things identify and distinguish communities. Through many interactions we acquire differentiated knowledge and skills for specialised and technical tasks, for work, for leisure and for social engagements.

A social practices curriculum is designed to socialise learners in differentiated discourses for community participation. The patterns of language – the discourses or texts – which characterise and distinguish social practices are basic units of analysis and organisation for a curriculum. Although the relationship of language use to social practices is not predetermined, there are expectations and conventions connected with language use for specific purposes.

Socialisation and Community Membership

Learning a language is learning to take part in community practices with language. Entry into new communities, into specialised spheres of human endeavour, requires awareness of specific social practices for participation (Wenger, 1998). For access to new spheres of human action, to new communities, people need to learn to use semiotic or meaning-making resources which characterise and distinguish communities. When children move into new spheres of human activity they use their acquired capacity for making meanings for the development of understandings for involvement in the new environments. A significant role of schooling is apprenticing children into the practices of selected communities, so that over time they learn the specialised language of sciences, for example, or the arts or environmental studies. Learners join groups for the purposes of engaging in common endeavours, for sharing, for learning and for fun in sporting teams, work coalitions, family celebrations or religious associations.

Learning additional languages is a process of socialisation. Learners are familiar with, and recognise, practices and related texts from daily participation in language-mediated or language-based experiences. With the advantage of prior experiences of meaning-making systems, learners draw upon their skills in the first language(s) in order to participate in communities with the meaning potential of another language system. As language has such a significant role in the mediation of cultural meanings, texts are central to learning participation in social practices. Participation in communities of practice means to understand and interpret signs and actions relevant to community actions and communication. Learning an additional language is about learning the meanings and value of signs for the identification, comprehension and expression of specific meanings. Language classes comprise communities where socialisation depends on teachers modelling texts for students – using language for building and sharing meanings in the conduct of classroom activities. In language classes the teacher's actions socialise learners from peripheral membership to fuller participation – during instructional conversations, in teaching content, in demonstrating and modelling language use, in jointly constructing new meanings, in problem-solving and in other language-mediated activities.

Social Practices and Texts

Social theory proposes that practices and texts constitute and enable human social behaviour (Figure 3.1). It foregrounds social practices and their texts in the design of a curriculum. The formation and operation of communities depend on people's ability to exchange and create meanings with language formulated as text.

People are involved in many communities distinguished by practices and ways of making meanings together. Significant social acts such as

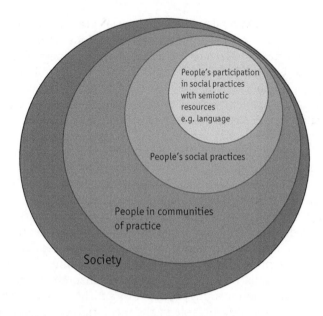

Figure 3.1 People's participation in society

forming and maintaining relationships, the transmission of experience and emotion as knowledge, joint action, planning and problem-solving are accomplished with texts. Texts are instances of language in use. Purposeful uses of language, whether spoken or written, involve the creation of coherent discourses. They are the language patterns for greeting and meeting, for teaching and planning, for entertaining, recounting and relating. Our socialisation develops discrimination and expectations about appropriate language choices and discourse conventions for maintaining and developing relationships.

Social theory foregrounds the social purposes of texts. Since a general purpose for learning languages is communication with community members, a social practices curriculum targets and identifies discourses for participation in selected practices. It identifies practices and their purposes. The social purpose of the student's email message (reproduced verbatim) in Text 3.1 is to apologise for late submission of an assignment for a university course. A formal teacher–student relationship is apparent in the form of address. It is accepted practice to explain late submission of assignments in our university courses. A medical certificate is justification for granting

To: Peter Mickan <peter.mickan@adelaide.edu.au>
Dear Dr. Mickan,
I am in your Thursday Language and Meaning Tutorial, unfortunately I am unwell today and can't come into to uni to hand in my third assignment. I do have a doctor's appointment and will attach a medical cerificate to my assignment when I hand it up tomorrow. I hope this is ok?
Regards, T

Text 3.1 Student email apology for late submission of an assignment

an extension. Communication through emails is normal. The form of this email is standard letter format adapted to the specific purpose, with address, identification and introduction, explanation, documentation, plan for submission, request for acknowledgement and greeting. An apparently simple email encodes information about our society (university education, subjects studied), relationships (teacher–student), services (medical practices) and social procedures (late submission of assignment). Cultural information and social purposes are enacted linguistically, not as separate dimensions but integrated as text. This is our experience of language use. A curriculum constructed with the texts of social practices is a practical way of working with language as social semiotic rather than as abstract grammar, taxonomies or strategies.

Language Learners' Experiences of Social Practices

Learners' socialisation in communities familiarises them with the purposes and practices of texts. They learn how to express different meanings from multiple encounters with language in social contexts. They have grown up with texts, observed their usefulness and used them in innumerable social interactions. They expand their textualising resources for participation in new practices when they encounter new contexts with different social phenomena. This occurs when they advance through school, enter new relationships, take on a new sport, go to work and change workplaces. Learners bring rich textual experiences to schooling which enable them to make sense of school discourses and to take part in new activities.

Learners of additional languages require specifically identified discourse resources to take part in practices of the target community. They recognise texts from prior experience and they interpret texts in the light of previous experience. They draw upon experiences and knowledge of texts for under-standing and conveying meanings. Where the social experiences of learners are familiar – schooling, playing games, carrying out tasks together – learners exploit first-language resources to take part in activities in a target language. They do not need to develop entirely new resources, because they are familiar with many of the features of language use: the selection of spoken or written forms, of appropriate genres, of degrees of familiarity and formality. More specifically, they will be familiar with the conventions of texts, with discourse conventions, such as responding to enquiries, taking turns in conversation, reading texts for meaning, listening and reacting to instructions, or protesting at an incursion into their habituated space. Based on previous experiences, learners will be concerned with and expect meaning as message in relation to context. To learn specific components of the target language, learners need intense analysis of the lexico-grammar of texts, together with opportunities for working with texts. Socialisation into the textual resources of additional languages proceeds from familiar language practices to new ones, and from social practices which require minimal language for making meanings to more language-dependent practices. Learners' experiences with texts equip them for participation in new contexts with new discourses. This is normal human experience. Learners utilise their accustomed discourse experiences to build language resources for engagement in new practices.

Engaging with Texts

Teaching with texts engages learners in making meanings. In speech and written language we textualise meanings. This is what learners are accustomed to do in their daily lives. When they hear or see language, they seek for meanings and they respond to meanings. They assume texts make sense. They are attuned to processing language to make sense of it.

The use of texts for teaching engages learners directly in the negotiation of potential meanings. Texts are comprehensible, contextualised resources for selective expression and purposeful composition of meanings. Building on learners' text and world knowledge, appropriately selected and prepared texts provide opportunities for making meanings: following the teacher's instructions, understanding narratives and composing reports. These are authentic engagements with language in use.

Working with texts directs attention to what is going on with language and how it is being used for the realisation of social purposes. The focus on language is in terms of its meaning potential. Learners develop awareness of different features of texts and their meanings through observation, reflection on and analysis of texts. For self-expression they borrow terms and phrases from other texts. They draw on the symbolic resources available in the texts of others – hearing and reading their texts – for the creation of their own texts.

Teaching Practices and Texts

Schools are socialisation sites for the development of literacy and numeracy practices. Studies of classroom talk and discipline discourses reveal the richness of language practices in education. A function of schooling is teaching new practices – spoken and written discourses for working together on tasks, for building relationships and for understanding phenomena of new school subjects, of new sporting skills, of new languages, of new music performances and artistic representations. Study of a subject such as science in school socialises learners into scientific practices. The same applies to learning to play chess, to measurement in mathematics, to classification in geography. Teachers use texts for many different purposes and in many different ways – for planning instruction, for whole-class readings and discussions, for group work and assessment, for individual tasks. Texts are the basis of teaching across the curriculum and are logical units for teachers to organise instruction. Working with texts is normal teaching practice.

With a social practice orientation, students engage in authentic tasks rather than artificial exercises. Teachers compose or select texts for students' use in class practices. The focus on text practices simplifies teachers' planning and preparation because students are accustomed to working with texts. With communicative and task-based pedagogies, teachers have to devote a lot of time to the preparation of materials for learners in their particular contexts in order to create relevant information-gap tasks, two-way tasks, problem-solving scenarios and other activities. Alternatively, they depend on externally produced textbooks with content – topics and tasks – not designed for local learners. Texts are practical organisers for classroom activities. If teachers choose the texts, this gives them flexibility in lesson planning. They can also adapt the curriculum to local circumstances and needs. Texts offer students choices in learning pathways. Language study is located in social practices as authentic experience.

A focus on social practices spells out purposes for language learning. We discuss, read, write, share, enjoy and work with texts. Texts package potential meanings for exploration in teaching. Socialisation of students takes place through work with authentic texts in shared book reading, reading for pleasure, solving problems, debating ideas, composing arguments and creating objects collaboratively. Socialisation includes text analysis –

the close study of how language choices influence and construct meaning potential. Texts give purpose and focus for classroom activities, eliminating the need to ask vacuous questions or carry on meaningless talk about pretend travel encounters.

The Grammar of Texts

The study of grammar in context is a big advantage of learning with texts. The analysis of written texts and transcripts of spoken language exposes the wordings which constitute potential meanings. Texts exhibit grammar as meaningful units for analysis. Learners observe and study language choices and variations in texts to understand how choices in grammar affect meanings in texts. A close examination of wordings of different texts reveals the effect of different lexico-grammatical choices on possible meanings, and exposes how variable combinations characterise functions or purposes of texts.

In a social theory curriculum, lexico-grammar and meaning are not segregated. Making meaning has precedence over the analysis of lexico-grammar. Language elements are integrated in texts as components for differentiating meanings. This is in contrast to traditional language education approaches, which separated analysis of form from meaning. Through the analysis of the lexico-grammar of texts, grammar is not separated from social function. A focus on form in texts makes transparent language selections for the realisation of social practices.

The purpose of text analysis is for students to recognise and use the lexico-grammar for their comprehension and the composition of texts. As all communities involve members in different practices, students learn to distinguish the lexico-grammar of different texts for different purposes. The procedure for the analysis of texts begins with exposure to texts in the contexts of social practices – with examination of purposes of texts in performance of practices. They note features which distinguish text types which fulfil specific social purposes. They identify generic structures – the sequences of events in texts. They highlight specific wordings which characterise the stages of texts. They mark out clauses, and examine clause structure and text cohesion. When speaking and writing, they adopt wordings from modelled texts and adapt them for expression of their meanings.

Texts for Different Practices

Educational programmes are designed to extend the textual practices of learners, so introducing students to new ways of doing and saying is core business. Social practices and texts are convenient organisers with which teachers can plan language programmes. Curriculum decisions relate directly to classroom activities: What are the social practices students need to learn to participate in? What are the language resources or texts for participation in those social practices? Teachers tailor content for the implementation of particular community practices. They select texts according to the social practice goals of learners.

The selection of practices and texts is flexible and adaptable to the specific needs and interests of learners and to institutional goals. Teachers select and write relevant texts for programmes with specific purposes, such as scientific or academic English. Texts are suitable for setting up resource-based learning, so students have access to selections of texts for self-study. Texts are convenient organisers for constructing work plans, for progression and sequencing of lessons and for assessment. Texts present learners with language sources to express their meanings.

Critical Literacy and Contestation

Texts comprise meaning potential. At the very heart of our language experience is the need to create our own meanings in response to texts. Texts set up opportunities for communication about content – for consent, for exploration of ideas and for contestation. Each interaction with texts involves processing the meanings of what is going on at a particular moment. We appraise and assess what we read, what we write, what we hear and say. In so doing, we declare, develop and define personal interpretations. Text encounters are opportunities for action – for expression of points of view, for argument, for dispute – and for negotiation, agreement, affirmation and confirmation. Texts are ideal for direct engagement of students in discussions as they constitute discourse resources for formulation of individual and group ideas.

Texts as expressions of culture embed values and ideologies with implicit social structures. The focus on the social practices of texts enables the analysis of options, power and positioning in discourses. Text analysis creates opportunities for dissection of arguments, for consideration of alternative interpretations of experiences, for expression of dissenting views and for reaching agreement on courses of action. We continuously assess or appraise what is going on around us. Encouraging critical analysis is a process of desirable dialogic interaction for learning meanings – for developing individual and group interpretations, and for the expression of personal points of view.

Summary

Texts are convenient units of analysis for teaching because they constitute a lot of human action. Learners are familiar with texts. They differentiate meanings and texts according to social purposes. Learners hear or see a text and attempt to understand it. They engage with texts as opportunities for making meanings. They formulate their own meanings with texts. Language learners select and segment recognisable language items in target-language texts in order to make sense of what is happening. They use recognisable elements to identify what is going on in social practices. Learners' familiarity with texts supports language learning as integrated, purposeful activity.

Notes and Readings

Language education is influenced by many theories of learning. The variety of theories regarding the acquisition of a second language can be quite confusing. Over the last two decades psycholinguistics theories have been particularly influential for communicative and for task-based language teaching. The concepts of input, interaction and output stem from these studies. Instead of introducing a variety of theories, the interest here is in socially contextualised learning. Socialisation theory has developed from documentation and analysis of the upbringing of children in different cultures and in different social contexts. Schieffelin and Ochs' (1986) work is particularly influential. Sociocultural theories in second-language education have been influenced by Vygotsky's (1968) work; he was a Russian social psychologist whose interest was in language and cognitive development in social environments. The view of language as a social semiotic under the influence of Halliday (see references) focuses on social relationships and language-mediated social practices. Halliday's (1994) systemic functional grammar has been applied to many aspects of education (Butt *et al.*, 2000; Eggins, 1994; Eggins & Slade, 1997; Martin & Rose, 2005, 2008; Unsworth, 2000). The metaphor of apprenticeship within communities of practice (Wenger, 1998) is useful for examining the specific practices and semiotic resources required for learning to become a member of particular social and work groups, including instructional classes.

Over the years, language teaching has adopted different units of analysis for construction of the curriculum. They include grammatical structures, speech acts, functions and notions, activities and tasks. The rationale for texts as units of analysis is well established in linguistics. I have argued elsewhere (Mickan, 2003, 2004) that the choice of text as a unit of analysis focuses instruction on making meanings. Feez (1998) argues for texts as the unit of analysis for syllabus design.

I have used the term 'text' to describe the language or discourses mediating social practices. Teaching with texts is not new to second-language teaching, because traditional academic foreign-language teaching involved the study of texts – novels, plays and poetry. For the few students who achieved higher levels of literacy in foreign languages, the literary analysis of foreign-language texts was most satisfying. Recent studies confirm the value of extensive reading of authentic texts for the development of proficiency in a second language. This is an argument for a text-based curriculum which engages learners in processing meaning in coherent oral and written discourses.

Tasks

(1) Record encounters with texts in normal situations. What texts do you use in the course of a day? What are the social practices the texts constitute?
(2) Survey a class to identify the texts they know and use in the course of a day.
(3) Document the main texts you use in a particular lesson. What are the social practices the texts are aligned with?
(4) Discuss with your students the texts they use in other lessons. Give the students a format for recording the texts used in different subjects in the curriculum. The following is an example of a format for recording texts used in a lesson:

Lesson (timetabled)	Subject	Classroom actions/ social practices	Text type	Comment
Lesson 3: 45 minutes	Biology	Listen to instructions, read diagram	Procedural text, diagram	Written, formal scientific

(5) Below is an email I received recently. What is the social purpose of the text? What wordings enable you to identify the purpose? What cultural information is embedded in the text? What is the structure of the text?

Dear Peter,
I'm in Donetsk right now, enjoying everything:) At the moment I'm observing two English language courses at different Universities, I think the already collected data will be useful for my research. However, I have not managed

to finish my final assignment for the Language Teaching in Specific Settings
course. If it is possible I would like to ask you for another week of extension.
I hope you are all right!
Thank you.
yours, K

(6) What are the implications for curriculum design of this statement
by Schieffelin and Ochs (1986: 183): 'Children acquire sociocultural
knowledge through exposure to and participation in everyday verbal
exchanges.'

4 Curriculum Design

A TEXT is an operational unit of language, as a sentence is a syntactic unit; it may be spoken or written, long or short; it includes as a special instance a literary text, whether haiku or Homeric epic. It is the text and not some super-sentence that is the relevant unit for stylistic studies; this is a functional-semantic concept and is not definable by size.
Halliday (1973: 107)

Introduction

This chapter describes the application of social theory to curriculum design. A curriculum is a framework for the planning and implementation of educational programmes. Essentially, education or training programmes have to do with induction, apprenticeship or further training in the practices of communities. Membership of communities is marked by some common purpose and shared use of semiotic resources and joint activities. The general aim of a curriculum is to provide opportunities for students to develop semiotic resources for participation in the social practices of communities. Its purpose is to structure educational activities so that resources, classroom practices and assessment are integrated for the realisation of a programme's goals.

Components of the Curriculum

Curriculum design begins with identification of a target community in which learners plan to work and communicate. The identified community might be an engineering class, a history class, a science class or a dance class. It might be a language class for learners of English, or Japanese or Korean. It might be a class learning English for academic purposes. Equally it might be an intensive in-service course in computer programming or bee-keeping. At the general level of syllabus specification, a community is identified together with the practices and resources which signify membership. Identification of a community situates students in contexts for working together as apprentices under the guidance of a teacher using meaning-making

43

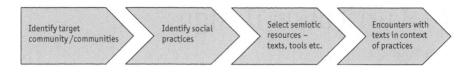

Figure 4.1 Designing a curriculum

resources. Newcomers gain membership of a community as they develop resources for working together.

The formal procedure for designing a curriculum centres on resources for participation in a specified community or communities of practice. The components of curriculum discussed in this chapter are framed according to the diagram shown in Figure 4.1, beginning with identification of a community which learners plan to join.

In social theory, the purpose of a curriculum is learners' development of meaning-making skills and knowledge for participation in specified cultural practices. Curriculum planners select and prioritise content and tasks for the implementation of a programme's goals. The units of analysis are social practices with texts of a community. The curriculum is structured with five core components (Figure 4.2).

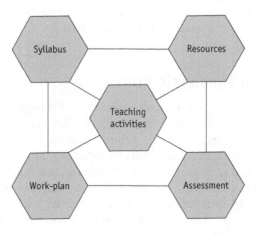

Figure 4.2 Core components of a curriculum

The core components of a curriculum are: syllabus, resources, work-plan, social practices and assessment.

- A **syllabus** sets out predetermined goals based on practices of a nominated community – electronic engineering, computing, graphic designing and so on. It serves as a map to guide programming for a work-plan, with programme goals, objectives and outcomes.
- A **work-plan** or teaching programme sequences teaching over time, with lesson plans and activities organised into units of work with a focus on practices and topics.
- **Resources** comprise the texts, tools and materials we use for making meanings and getting things done in a community (i.e. these are semiotic resources).
- **Teaching activities** (as a form of social practice) describe working with learners as apprentices with texts and other semiotic resources for developing the potential for making meanings in a community.
- **Assessment** is based on students' formulation of specific meanings in targeted types of text.

Syllabus

A syllabus sets out the goals of a programme – the aims and objectives of a programme for a particular group of learners. A syllabus might include learning outcomes as well. A syllabus is often externally prepared and monitored, as with a national curriculum and with external assessment schemes. Where the curriculum or syllabus is predetermined as part of a national policy or an institutional programme, teachers prepare teaching plans based on a prescribed syllabus. Where a teacher has discretion over a programme, the teacher has the opportunity to plan and develop a local syllabus. Where a teacher bases instruction on a textbook, this serves as the curriculum. The extent to which teachers adhere to a syllabus varies. Some educational systems and schools expect strict adherence to a detailed syllabus, while others give teachers responsibility for preparation of their own teaching programmes following general guidelines.

Aims, objectives and outcomes

Aims, objectives and outcomes guide planning and programming for teachers and learners.

- The **aims** of the programme state its (social) purposes. In some situations the syllabus for a language curriculum describes 'communication' as the aim. For practical purposes, such a broad aim needs to be more specific: communicate in which community, with whom, for what purposes, how or in what modality, and at what level, to note a few considerations. Specificity is achieved through description of a community and through stating objectives as practices learners will take part in.

- The **objectives** describe learners' participation in social practices. The objectives specify text conventions for engagement in social practices.
- The **outcomes** are based on objectives. They specify learners' participation and progression in a structured programme – what language practices learners will be able to take part in by the end of a programme or unit of work. Outcomes provide teachers and students with measures of progress towards goals. For teachers they provide a standard for

---

Box 4.1 Syllabus outline for an intensive study programme

Study programme: Intensive four-week course on English as a second language
This course, held in Adelaide, South Australia, was designed for a student group from Japan. The students were in their first year at university and had joined the study tour to improve their spoken English. Their standard of spoken English was basic.

Aims
(1) To develop students' proficiency in spoken English.
(2) To introduce students to aspects of South Australian people and places through the use of English.

Objectives
(1) To participate in classroom events (e.g. follow classroom instructions, take part in class tasks).
(2) To present an oral report and prepare a written report on a visit to the Cleland Wildlife Park.
(3) To describe the process of making wine at a South Australian winery.
(4) To write a report on a shopping visit to the Central Market in Adelaide.

Outcomes
(1) Participation in the practices of the class.
(2) Oral report on a visit to wildlife park and report in a journal.
(3) Report on a visit to a winery with a description of the procedure for making wine.
(4) Description of a shopping excursion.

assessment or testing. For students they provide a map detailing interim progression, or milestones towards a goal, as well as a sense of making progress as they experience achievement through participation in practices.

Box 4.1 presents an example constructed for an overseas study programme, with only the main aims, objectives and outcomes described. The students for this programme were Japanese undergraduates with little experience of talking in English, although they had studied English for a number of years. The main aim of the programme was for students to experience spoken English in an English-speaking city. Activities were organised with tour directors, so that the programme integrated language experiences with local sightseeing. Lesson activities were designed for students to talk and write about their experiences related to living in Adelaide with host families and working with the teacher and with other students. Students used the English language in lessons, for reporting on experiences, for describing procedures and observations. For the study programme the core texts included:

- copies of transcripts of classroom practices – discourse with a focus on teacher instructions; group-work talk; requesting clarification and assistance; initiating enquiries as well as responding to enquiries;
- examples of oral reports, with transcripts, on visits to the wildlife park;

Table 4.1 Text-based syllabus with outcomes

Aims	Objectives	Outcomes
Enjoy narratives	To listen to the teacher reading modern stories while following written text; to comment on stories	Understand stories; share responses to stories; take pleasure in making sense of texts
Participate in classroom tasks	To understand and respond to the teacher's instructions	Act on the teacher's oral/written instructions in class
Conduct group-work tasks in the target discourses	To use the target language to work together on group tasks	Group-work completion through appropriate use of language
Report on a school sports match	To read models of reports; to compose a written report on a school sports match	Report on sports match for a class magazine

- procedural texts illustrating the processes of grape production and wine production;
- descriptions of tourist destinations around Adelaide.

Another way to set out the syllabus is with a focus on the outcomes (as opposed to aims and objectives, above), with specification of the social practices and texts learners are expected to participate in at the end of a sequence of activities or lessons. Table 4.1 presents an example of how this might be done for a school-based programme. A syllabus set out in this way provides a simplified overview of content to be covered in a unit of work or series of lessons. Describing outcomes is particularly useful for learners to develop study plans and to plot their progress. It is also useful for negotiating the curriculum – for teachers to consult with students about the content of a programme.

A formal curriculum for external assessment: Goals and outcomes

The following example of a text-based curriculum is from the official assessment authority in South Australia, the Senior Secondary Assessment Board of South Australia (SSABSA), which prepares curriculum documents for the South Australian Certificate of Education (SACE). The documents guide teaching and assessment work for students taking English as a second language (ESL). The curriculum states that 'Language is regarded as a resource for conveying meaning' (SSABSA, 2006: 1). The analysis of texts is based on systemic functional grammar, with language examined in contexts with reference to field, tenor and mode (Eggins, 1994; Halliday, 1994). The study of texts is constructed around students' use of English appropriate to specific contexts. For example, students are given the following advice for Stage 1 of the programme:

> In Stage 1 English as a Second Language, students develop their ability to use English that is accurate and appropriate in a variety of contexts. They read, view, and listen to short texts, and discuss issues of interest. Students develop their skills in delivering effective oral presentations without undue reliance on memorized or written text. Students are given the opportunity to draft and edit written work in consultation with their teacher. They undertake research and interact with other people in the community. Throughout the program the structure and language patterns appropriate to various speaking and writing situations are taught and modeled, especially those in formal contexts. (SSABSA, 2006: 3)

The document goes on to give a statement of goals (SSABSA, 2006: 5):

These subjects are designed to develop students':
- ability to read, listen to, and obtain information from a variety of texts, including electronic;
- ability to speak and write with clarity, accuracy, and appropriateness for a range of audiences and purposes, and in a range of contexts, using technology where appropriate;
- ability to communicate effectively with other people, taking into consideration the social and cultural contexts of the situation;
- knowledge of the language structures and features of English, and ability to apply this knowledge in the construction of texts;
- critical understanding of the wider cultural references in texts (references to other texts or cultural events or important people);
- awareness of their own identity and their capacity to participate in a multicultural society.

It also gives a statement of learning outcomes (SSABSA, 2006: 10):

At the end of the program in Stage 1 English as a Second Language, students should be able to:
- understand aspects of the relationship between contexts and texts;
- compose texts in a variety of genres;
- obtain and evaluate information and opinions from a range of written, oral, visual, and electronic texts;
- exchange opinions and convey information and experiences in a limited range of formal and informal situations;
- demonstrate clear and accurate language skills when writing, reading, speaking, and listening.

This is an example of a formal, institutional curriculum constructed around texts and text-based tasks. Teachers use the curriculum to plan teaching programmes, to create activities and to evaluate achievement. The focus on textual practices provides a framework for designing educational programmes in general, and for specific-purpose courses, for study programmes and for excursions. For students, the syllabus provides guidance for working in the programme.

Resources for Developing Meaning Potential

Social theory assumes that students:

- will work with many practice-related texts;
- will understand and use many relevant texts over time;
- will compose and use their own texts as they gain expertise in community discourses.

Resources comprise the texts, tools and materials for making meanings and getting things done in a community. The selection of resources is based on the goals and objectives of a programme. Institutional discourses are ready-made teaching resources for natural, situated work with texts. The texts are practical and accessible resources for teaching. Making the language of these interactions visible is an obvious starting point for the selection of texts.

Classes of students working in lessons comprise communities. Lessons are settings managed naturally with texts. Work is largely conducted through predictable discourses, which fulfil organisational functions such as management, content teaching and social exchanges. Such language practices are also common to many workplaces. Formal discourses include video-recordings with transcriptions of students' talk with teachers and with other students, topic- and subject-related texts, news, fiction and faction. Recordings with transcriptions of informal talk, of students chatting, of workplace talk, of arguments and discussions might be negotiated. Students' group work on tasks provides discourses for analysis of collaboration, planning and processes for task completion. Student documentation and transcription of talk develops awareness of discourse resources for activities.

Subject-specific teaching incorporates texts comprising subject content. Science texts, for example, include information about topics: introductions to topics; procedures for conducting experiments; instructions about laboratory safety protocols; reports. With socialisation into new subjects and new language practices, the teacher expands the repertoire of texts: texts for the study of new subjects (diagrams and descriptions of T-rays in electronic engineering), texts for doing new activities (following instructions for the use of lasers), texts for reporting research (academic article in a journal in electronic engineering), computer programs for meta-programming for software evolution. The selection of texts meets programme goals and is adjusted to the levels of learning and to the prior experiences and interests of students. Selection builds upon learners' current experiences of discourse, so that even for beginners there is a choice of texts. Without the rigid sequencing of items as in a grammar-based syllabus, teachers have options to choose and negotiate preferred texts.

Over time, teachers collate multiple resources and compile text banks, which can be made available for students' self-access. Texts range from letters to integrated, multimodal texts with full audio, visual and kinetic dimensions. Teachers write texts for and with their students and in web-linked contexts access oral and written texts electronically. Text banks offer teachers and students choices for action, for analysis and for fun. With a range of texts, classes have resources for individual study, for extension work and for negotiation of learning pathways.

Work-Plans and Teaching Programmes

Syllabuses provide maps for teachers writing work-plans or programmes sequenced as lessons and activities organised into units of work. A teaching programme describes an action plan for a class or classes over a period of time, organised with teaching topics and class activities. It includes lesson plans, units of work and programmes for a term, semester, year or level of study (basic, intermediate, advanced). In some educational contexts, teachers' programmes are prescribed in syllabuses and textbooks for public examinations. Even in such situations teachers have discretion over the use of classroom time to meet national programme goals and also to broaden students' experiences. For example, a reduction in time spent on grammatical exercises increases the time for reading and composing texts for meaning, which integrates the teaching of the language system, that is, the grammar, with meaning-making activities (Lim, 2007). In other contexts teachers have responsibility for the programme content and plan according to institutional requirements and learners' prior experiences and aspirations. The programme proposals in this chapter assume that a teacher has responsibility for lesson planning and unit planning. Lesson and unit plans describe teachers' intended instructional actions in a course of study so that there is cohesion and direction in instruction. Such programmes of work guide teachers' instruction and give learners direction for self-management of study tasks. Figure 4.3 sets out a suggested procedure for organising lessons and units of work.

Previous experiences of texts

The first consideration for unit and lesson planning are learners' internalised discourse skills developed from multiple language encounters. The challenge is to harness these skills for learning additional languages. Learners are familiar with purposeful discourses. They know that different modes of language serve different purposes, and choose when and what to

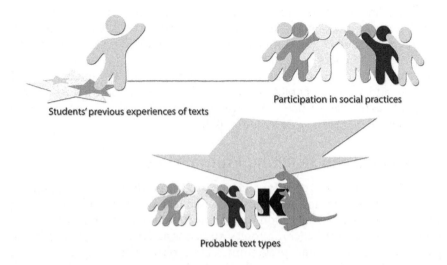

Figure 4.3 Procedure for developing work-plans, lessons and activities

read, write or talk about. They have conversational skills for turn-taking and pausing and for differentiating requests from greetings, questions from answers. All this experience is the basis for structuring a programme from known texts to new texts and to text variants. The aim is to expand learners' familiarity with particular text types and variations of text types and to broaden their use of text types. The selection of texts is planned to extend learners' comprehension and production of texts. Students are socialised into more complex and new language practices by broadening their textual experiences.

Participation in social practices

Step 2 is the identification of the social practices of a target or group in which students wish to participate. For example, in subject-specific or content-based classes, students are preparing to take part in the activities and the associated discourses of members of the subject – historians, electronic engineers, bio-technologists, or whoever. In general language classes, the target community is the language class and its activities.

Language practices and probable texts

The teaching programme is structured around practices and texts. Students need to use selected texts for participation in practices. Teachers identify practices and texts for the organisation of lessons and units of work. Table 4.2 sets out a segment of a work-plan structured around a class community, social practices and probable texts. The purpose is for students to research information on the habitat and diet of kangaroos in an elementary science class. The example indicates a few of the practices and discourses associated with a class study in science. It suggests that class activities require students to know and use multiple types of text to carry out practices. Texts are resources for students to do things together. The aims and the practices of the activity focus students' attention on different text types. The teacher's task is to support students' text encounters, including analysis of the wordings of text exemplars for obtaining information and for the formulation of reports. The purpose is for learners to access the resources and gain lexico-grammatical awareness for textualising meanings about kangaroos.

Programmes of work introduce students to new social practices with their technical and variable discourses. Our language practices involve choice at the level of register: whether to use spoken language or written language; whether to use mixed visual and verbal modes; whether to use informal or formal discourse; whether to use common or technical terminology. Formal meetings sometimes commence with informal chatter before written agendas and documents are discussed. In homes and workplaces language use ranges from general to more specialised discourses, as we continually adjust our discourse to different social purposes. Units of work are plans for widening the uses of spoken and written language as students take part in an increasing range of language practices.

Table 4.2 Planning a component or unit of a work-plan

Aims for class members	Social practices	Probable text types
To study habitat and diet of kangaroos and present information to another class	Planning study of kangaroos; searching for information; selecting and recording information; organising information for a PowerPoint presentation; editing report; presenting report	Transcript of planning discussion; examples/models of similar studies on other animals; multimodal texts for research in library, online, interviews; texts in books, articles, pictures; notes for presentation of the report; PowerPoint – presentation of oral and written information

Teaching Activities

Activities describe the work teachers do with students in order to build students' abilities to participate in programme practices. Activities include working with varieties of texts, analysis of characteristic discourse features of texts, and production of texts. Text-based activities are all meaning-making. In Figure 4.4 I have outlined a framework for the preparation of instructional material.

The aim of classroom activities is for students to experience and observe language in action. Teaching focuses on development of students' abilities to make meanings. The focused and selective analysis of the language of social practices prepares students for the expression of their own meanings with language. Understanding the meanings of texts and expressing meanings in texts is central to teaching. Preparation of teaching materials does not require dismantling of language from context with the extraction of meaning, so the language does not have to be recontextualised and meaning reinjected for classroom use. Instruction begins with text types and content with which learners are familiar, so that they use their discourse and world knowledge for the prediction of meanings and for learning patterns of language in use. These are texts with recognisable layouts and spatial designs (lists, advertisements, procedures) and familiar topics, with accompanying illustrations.

The structuring and sequencing of teaching activities mixes spoken and written modes, as in story reading. For example, learners listen to the teacher reading a story and follow the written text of the story at the same time. Learners observe the teacher's use of language, witnessing language in action. Lessons are spaces for modelling and observing language practices,

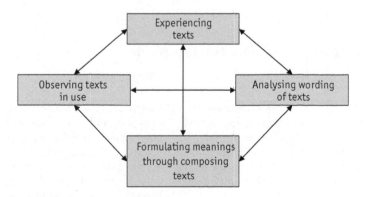

Figure 4.4 Working with texts for meaning-making

including close analysis of texts for learners to see how texts work to make meanings. Learning new discourses requires conscious attention to the features characteristic of text types or genres, so that students choose from the language system the lexico-grammar for understanding and expressing ideas. Explicit attention to the language of texts reveals for learners the selections and choices for expression of experiences and documentation of information. They observe how different choices or selections of wordings serve different social purposes. The analysis of the grammar of the language system is not separated from use. The study of the grammar is based on the text as part of practices.

Assessment

The criteria for assessment are described in terms of texts and the specific features of texts. It is the purpose of language learning (and thus testing) to be able to use language in appropriate ways. Therefore tests are designed to rate performance based on students' realisation of meanings in texts through appropriate discourse and lexico-grammatical selections. A text-based approach describes specific discourse or text features for the assessment of texts. It recognises the integration of discourse semantic and lexico-grammatical resources, which determine the appropriateness and fluency of a text. The criteria then are based upon the social purposes of texts and the language used for the realisation of those social purposes.

Summary

In this chapter I have outlined the main features of a curriculum. As the curriculum is structured with practices and texts, teachers and students have ready-made teaching materials for working with language, for the comprehension and composition of spoken and written language. The chapters which follow go into more detail about teaching activities, text analysis and planning units of work.

Notes and Readings

The curriculum design outlined in this chapter provides a procedure for language policy development, for language planning and for curriculum construction. For national or state curriculum writers, the plan sets out a principled and at the same time practical framework for centrally designed programmes. Where teachers are at liberty to develop their own programmes or work within the boundaries of externally mandated programmes they will create programmes responsive to students' needs. Writers can apply the model to programmes with different purposes and for different levels of education. There is a useful introduction to syllabus design by Feez (1998).

Tasks

(1) Plan a short teaching unit structured according to the design in Figure 4.3. Set out a sequence of lessons with texts: consider what texts learners are familiar with, what social practices you want students to take part in, and what texts they will need to develop.

(2) Textbooks are often used to organise the teaching of programmes. The books serve the purpose of a curriculum. Evaluate a language teaching textbook. What concept(s) of language learning can you identify in the book? Is the content of the book consistent with teaching aims or goals? For example, if the book aims to teach students to write academic English, do students work with academic language texts? They should be reading, observing and analysing authentic texts before being expected to write their own.

(3) Review and list the texts in a textbook with which you are familiar. Analyse the texts in terms of authenticity and relevance to students. This task could be carried out with students in a language class.

(4) Students are often set group-work tasks. Such events are practical opportunities to use the target language purposefully. To work in groups, students need discourse models appropriate to the task. Students record group work and analyse the discourse for working together in the target language; use the recordings and transcripts as exemplars for students to speak together, drawing on phrases in the transcripts to express their own meanings.

(5) If you are teaching with a centrally determined, grammatical syllabus, review and analyse it in terms of practices and texts. What texts could be selected to implement the aims of the syllabus? For example, if one aim is 'to take part in simple conversations', review the purpose of a 'simple conversation'.

(6) The curriculum for language teaching is very often prescriptive, requiring teachers to follow in detail programmes of work, leaving little room for negotiation. The scope for spontaneous activities may be limited. Review the curriculum to identify texts which meet syllabus specifications and at the same time interest teachers and students.

(7) Analyse task-based and text-based curriculum designs. How are the designs similar and how do they differ?

5   Curriculum Planning

A key insight of genre theory is that language occurs in a social context and that it is structured according to the purposes it serves in a particular context and according to the social relations entailed by that activity.
Callaghan *et al.* (1993: 181)

Introduction

The practical side of curriculum design is planning a programme. The purpose of a curriculum plan is the selection and sequencing of activities for the apprenticeship of learners into selected practices and uses of texts. Teachers have opportunities to adapt and create programmes appropriate to the needs, aspirations and interests of students. They have opportunities to create programmes with texts based on a framework of practices and texts which comply with departmental guidelines and national or state policies. Of most importance for the design of a curriculum is clarity of purpose for learners. Curriculum designers set out specific social purposes and language practices connected to learners' aspirations.

Planning a programme of work is a creative activity. A programme identifies practices and discourses for addressing students' need for participation in a work group or community. Figure 5.1 proposes a planning procedure. The purpose of a programme is to mentor students for participation in targeted practices. Planning begins with the identification of a target community and practices which define and characterise the group. The needs of learners are described in terms of resources – the knowledge and skills required for membership of the group. Students join a class in which interactions around lesson activities apprentice them as members and develop and enhance their practices. Analysis of language is integrated into encounters with text practices. The following sections detail the planning procedure set out in Figure 5.1.

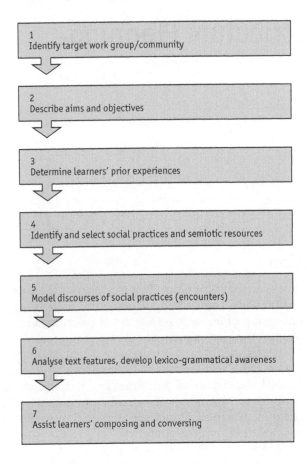

Figure 5.1 Programme planning procedure (adapted from Mickan, 2006)

Identification of Target Community and Social Practices

Curriculum design begins with a description of what learners need to know and do to take part in specific community practices. People's relationships encompass many communities, which overlap and intertwine. A community might be a formal class – professional, knowledge-based and technical – or it might be an informal leisure group of people who ride bikes, play chess or spend time chatting with long-term friends. People come together for shared activities, for work, and/or for knowledge and skills development. Identification of a target community is a selective process. Instruction encompassing a range of possible communities requires prioritising practices and texts. Choice is guided by analysis of the following:

- What community is significant for learners' goals?
- What are the language practices learners need and desire to develop?
- What potential language conventions, that is, texts or genres, constitute the practices?

A work group or class is a community of contact, whether an engineering or philosophy class, a group learning English for specific purposes (ESP) or English for academic purposes (EAP), a study tour or an art programme. Taking part in the practices of a class community is a priority. Classroom discourse is varied and purposeful, rich with opportunities for mentoring and rehearsing participation; discourses include authentic, essential and useful samples of language from communities outside of lessons and schools. Lessons, in fact, are appropriate contexts for communication in a target language, since people come together with the shared purpose of gaining skills and knowledge.

A plan of instruction specifies a community or communities, selects practices and chooses representative texts which characterise participation, as in Table 5.1. In content-based teaching, actions and subject matter – the epistemology, the knowledge and skills which constitute a subject or discipline – define practices, texts and roles. For the design of a history programme, for example, we can ask what it is that historians do, that is, what their practices are (e.g. record events, interpret past experiences

Table 5.1 Two examples of target communities, with practices and related discourses

Target community	Practices for focus	Representative or potential texts
Meat processors in abattoirs	Supervisor's instructions; team work; safety instructions	Supervisor's talk, with transcripts, exemplars of work-group talk, workplace safety instructions
Engineering firm	Consultation with clients, planning with colleagues, drafting project plans, evaluation of project, preparation of reports	Transcripts of consultations and planning, exemplars of draft projects, evaluations and reports

and events; search for and evaluate evidence) and what discourses they use (documentation of events, descriptions, composing arguments as evidence). The purpose is to select and state with as much precision as possible the work and discourses of historians so that teaching socialises learners initially as amateur historians and over time as professional historians.

We are able to join in the practices of different communities because our discourses are built with language elements from many different encounters. The intertextuality or composite nature of texts means that instruction in one context has generalisable and transferable resources across domains and sectors of human activity. The foundation of our learning is the ability to transfer our know-how to different practices in different contexts using the Lego-like or elastic capacity of the language system to interlock the lexico-grammar in varied patterns for the expression of multiple and novel meanings.

Describe Aims and Objectives

The aims of a programme are influenced by factors internal and external to a class community. The planning process should take account of the following:

- **the prior experiences and social needs of students** – familiarity with social practices and discourses and social requirements for participation in a community or a work group;
- **semiotic resources** – texts, materials and tools central to participation in community practices;
- **the tasks or practices** required for students' socialisation through concentrated work with those semiotic resources;
- **work-plan** – progression and sequencing of work;
- **outcomes** – details of expected outcomes.

Planning takes account of institutional policies, guidelines and goals, the needs and aspirations of learners, and individual teacher preferences in negotiation with learners.

Determine Learners' Prior Experiences and Their Familiarity with Social Practices

The selection and then the prioritising of practices draw upon students' previous experiences, their familiarity with social practices and discourses, and specifically their knowledge of relevant texts. The purposes are:

(1) to ascertain practices and texts which learners are able to recognise and comprehend (for example, familiar texts such as an advertisement, a narrative, a recount, a report);

(2) to determine learners' capacity to predict discourses associated with specific practices;

(3) to select and organise practices with the support of recognisable and relevant texts.

The process capitalises on learners' accumulated knowledge of practices and their discourses. It creates continuities across contexts. It recognises what students already know about social participation and the semiotic resources for participation.

Table 5.2 is a brief account of the first few minutes of an initial seminar for a postgraduate EAP class. The class was a new community, but the members were not newcomers to academic study. Most students had studied English as an additional language for their first degree. When I walked into the room the students were seated at tables in a semi-circle with the front table kept free for me to sit at. They were chatting but on my entry they stopped talking. I greeted the students and as it was a new class

Table 5.2 Students' knowledge of practices and discourses of an introductory academic class

Recorded practices	Knowledge of practices and discourses
Students seated in semi-circle with front table unoccupied They stopped talking when I entered They turned to face me They greeted me	Participants familiar with social structures and relationships, with conventional teacher/student roles and classroom practices within tertiary education
I asked students to introduce themselves in turn, as this was a new class Students introduced themselves individually around the class The first student gave name and place of origin and then other students imitated this format of introduction	Students responded – familiar with speech convention of self-introduction to group of strangers in relatively formal language
I handed out a study guide with an outline of the course I directed discussion on sections of text	Familiarity with academic practices and pedagogies: students' knowledge of status of text, of need to listen to lecturer

asked the students to introduce themselves. After a few moments' silence one student introduced herself and then each followed in turn, basing individual introductions on the first person's text. After the introductions I handed out the course programme and began to explain the purposes of and the practices planned for the course. From the moment I entered the room, I observed students' familiarity with the conventional practices of a university seminar: how to exchange meanings by responding to instructions, by doing tasks and by working together. Students selected practices and semiotic resources appropriate to participation in a situated literacy event – a university seminar. The example suggests the need for a broad concept of prior knowledge. The ability to recognise practices and their texts assists newcomers to training programmes or academic courses.

Identify and Select Social Practices and Semiotic Resources

Social practices are people's acts of living and working in communities. People develop practices in their relationships with other people. The analysis of social practices takes account of the features listed in Box 5.1. Identification of a community or communities guides the selection of characteristic practices. In school settings an analysis of what is taught provides a focus for the identification of practices specific to communities. In content subjects – mathematics, history, biology, physical education – we

---

Box 5.1 Social practices (adapted from Mickan, 2006: 12–13)

- People's actions in community comprise social practices. People engage in multiple, interrelated, multimodal and ever-changing practices in ongoing encounters in communities.
- Social practices are semiotic events. Participation in social practices requires comprehension of and response to what is going on. Human orientation in social practices is towards the meanings of experiences and the meanings of people's actions – towards making sense of the present, of the past and of the future.
- People's participation situates social practices in time and place.
- People attribute cultural significance to practices according to functions in society.
- People's engagement in social practices integrates physical activity, cognitive processing and the material world.

are able to identify specific practices which comprise the subject. We learn to understand and to take part in practices through our relationships and communication with community members. Learners join a science class, for example, and learn the practices and discourses of beginner scientists. Through participation in these practices of a science class, children observe, use and develop the semiotic resources for participation. Lessons create opportunities for participation in reading about the history of scientific discoveries, in reading about and observing experiments, and in reporting science experiments (Mickan, 2007). Similarly in a language class, members are involved in many practices: acting on the teacher's instructions, conversing, enquiring, working together, presenting homework, documenting activities and so on. A curriculum lists customary community practices and potential discourses for conducting them.

What semiotic resources?

Membership of communities is marked by distinctive practices, which are carried out with semiotic resources and tools, with language as a preeminent semiotic: the creation, maintenance and renewal of culture are dependent on literacy and oracy practices. Some practices we conduct without language. For other practices, such as computer science or coaching

Table 5.3 Class-based examples of social practices and texts

Social practices and aims	Objectives	Text resources
Participation in classroom work: to participate in lesson practices; to complete group tasks	To understand and respond to the teacher's instructions; to work together on class tasks	Teacher discourses; transcripts of teacher talk (class management, subject content, instructions, social interactions); transcripts + video-clips of group-work talk
Story telling: to enjoy listening to and reading narratives; to respond to stories	To understand stories read by the teacher and other students; to react to and comment on a story	Narratives in big-book format or electronic versions for whole-class reading; audio-recorded stories for individual listening and reading
News: to watch/listen to the news; to become familiar with current affairs	To understand selected news items	Newspaper texts; transcripts of radio news; web-based news reports; television news with transcripts/video-streaming

sport, we use material objects and physical activity with language. Many of our daily actions are conducted with language, both as a determinant of actions and as shaped by actions. Identification of social practices provides the practical information for the selection of the semiotic resources needed for participation in the chosen community – for choosing discourses for participation in language-mediated practices. Spoken and written texts provide instances or examples of language in context with the lexico-grammatical resources for participation in activities. A class-based example is presented in Table 5.3. Where multimedia resources are available, texts can be presented in different modalities, with visual and sound technologies to enhance contextual information for comprehension of what is going on.

Social Practices (Encounters)

We learn to take part in social practices from frequent, intensive socialisation experiences with other people, with human artefacts (e.g. books, models, computers) and with the physical/material environment. Growing up is marked by participation in increasingly more specialised communities with distinctive ways of doing things. We observe this in workplaces when new appointees commence initial duties and over time manage more complex tasks. In the school curriculum, subject specialisation increases through primary school to secondary school, and students select subjects and pathways related to interests and career options. Learners' participation in social practices extends their awareness of meanings, increases their comprehension of discourses and expands the resources for expression of meanings. Instruction focuses on contact with language in use together with explicit analysis of language in use. I have highlighted the integration of language resources with social practices in the following three 'context' examples.

Context 1: Science class

This first example (Mickan, 2007) is from a science class for ESL learners. A study of science lessons identified selected practices which were characteristic of apprenticing students into a science class in a high school.

Science lesson plan

Community: Secondary-school science class was a community for apprenticing students into the practices of elementary science.
Aim: to conduct an experiment in science – procedures for participation in scientific activities.

Semiotic resources: oral language, textbook procedure for conduct of experiment, diagrams in science book, laboratory benches, equipment.
Approach: participation in science practices through literacy events and lab work.
Social practices: the class took part in multiple practices, including:
- following instructions in the textbook;
- interpreting diagrams for doing science experiments;
- setting up a science experiment;
- conducting a science experiment in a science laboratory;
- interpreting the results of the experiment;
- documenting the experiment.

The following transcribed exchange (from Mickan, 2007) took place between the teacher (T) and two students (S and ST) who had finished the experimental procedure:

> ... the teacher gives instructions for cleaning up and putting the equipment away. He uses and repeats terms connected with the experimental procedure.

T ... What do you do after it is boiled?
S First to knock the fire off and then let the temperature down.
T Let the solution cool. After letting it cool, what do you do, ST?
ST Take two receptacles ... and then put some um, how do you say? ... the actual colour ... the solution....
T Do you know what decant means?
ST Pour. pour. pour the liquid.
T This picture is showing decanting [pointing to illustration in the book]. So it's pouring liquids and keeping solids in the beaker ... so just letting the liquid go out.

The teacher prompts students to talk about the experimental processes. A student's informal but correct response ('First to knock the fire off and then let the temperature down') is reformulated by the teacher with a clause typical of school science reporting ('Let the solution cool'). The exchange continues as the teacher scaffolds the students' explanations. The focus on use of specific terms and on the sequencing of processes ('After letting it cool, what do you do, ST?') is another preparatory step for writing up the experiment. This final part of the lesson incorporates discourse from the textbook and from previous explanations, adding to students' experiences of discourse related to activities underway.

Multiple, connected encounters with practices and texts were recorded in the high-school science programme from which the extract comes. In such encounters learners experience the integration of different meaning-making resources for carrying out tasks. Working together, students experienced and used language as a resource for making meanings.

Context 2: German as a foreign language class – writing narratives

The second example (Mickan, 2000) comes from a study of a class in German as a foreign language. Senior secondary students were in their fourth year of study in a largely grammar-based programme. Students wrote texts on topics nominated by the teacher in addition to oral communicative tasks and written grammatical exercises. The study documented individual students' composing of report, narrative and letter texts, with notes and recordings of verbal protocols. Within the complexity of the composing process, two features of students' composing texts are relevant. The example is of the composition of a narrative by one particular student (AC).

AC approached writing a narrative in German as unproblematic. As he wrote he commented:

> I'm trying to figure out what to write; I'm trying to think what will happen immediately after; not so much the German, it's the story.

AC's prior experience and knowledge of narratives are a key resource for composing in German. He was particularly conscious of the social purpose of what he was writing – to entertain:

> To make it sound more like a story and not a series of facts.

Although AC was constrained in what he was able to express in German, his attention to correct grammar and word choice was within his overarching wish to write an interesting story. AC attended to grammar and word selection in the context of the text and according to the purpose of the narrative – to enhance the narrative. AC's search for vocabulary displays not so much his lack of a German lexicon, but rather his desire for specificity through lexical choices which will express his narrative intentions.

AC and other students in the German class integrated social purpose, text type and grammatical selections as they composed texts. From prior socialisation they had internalised critical elements of different text types. Students revealed previous discourse experiences in their orientation to the purposes of different types of text. This was an example of building upon the semiotic resources of earlier experiences for expression of meanings in another language.

Context 3: Postgraduate applied-linguistics class

In this final example (Teramoto & Mickan, 2008), Hiromi, a postgraduate student from Japan, reflected on her experiences of writing a first assignment (critical review) for one of the courses in applied linguistics at the University of Adelaide. For the assignment, students were asked to review research on a topic. The class instruction read as follows:

Assignment One: Topic Review

Due date: Friday April 11

Select a topic for critical review. Read current and relevant research and related literature on the topic and present this as a written and oral report to the class. It is suggested that you work with a partner in researching and presenting the topic. Suggested topics are listed below. Others may be negotiated.

- Communicative language teaching
- Task-based language teaching
- Genre-based language teaching
- Language awareness
- Bilingual language teaching
- Immersion language teaching programs
- Literacy practices.

Hiromi analysed her own practices in preparing for and writing the assignment. They included:

- understanding the task – what are the meanings of 'critical' and 'review'?
- making sense of and choosing a topic – requires knowledge of domain or field;
- interpreting the topic – literacy indicates something to do with reading and writing;
- electronic skills and knowledge – internet search, selection of electronic references and recognition of relevant details;
- referencing system;
- making notes from readings – understanding, foregrounding, selection, copying;

- consulting with lecturer – framing questions, expressing ideas, understanding responses;
- teamwork – collaboration over how, what and so on;
- framing theoretically the review – social practices;
- composing a response – selecting the appropriate type of text, organising scribbles into a review, deciding how to quote from references, elaborating points of view, adopting points of view, reshaping concepts of literacy;
- editing – proofreading and responding to edits;
- reflection on the task – how to make it visible and a technical lens through which to examine actions;
- final report – structured and edited.

Hiromi depicted the technical complexity of academic practices, in this case writing an assignment. She wrote that, in the process of preparing and writing the assignment, 'I was gaining awareness that through learning the content of a subject, learners are engaged in multiple social practices simultaneously intertwined with multiple roles in achieving multiple goals' (Teramoto & Mickan, 2008: 9). The task was planned as an academic introduction of students into the topic of language learning in applied linguistics. The task assumed multiple practices, which were not spelt out for students. The reflections of Hiromi make clearer the complexity of practices students are expected to acquire in the course of their work, and the difficulty of identifying the separate practices required. Hiromi learned about literacy practices while preparing for and composing the assignment: 'while some of the ideas I gained were contingent upon the assignment task, others were generated through participation in the practices for realising the task and from reflections on them' (Teramoto & Mickan, 2008: 9). For Hiromi, the assignment required engagement in multiple practices, requiring management of a variety of quite different discourses.

Text Analysis and Grammatical Awareness

A curriculum plan includes the selection of texts for an analysis of their grammatical features. Grammar is taught as components of texts – within the context of the specific purposes of texts. The analysis of the language system is not separated from use, as in traditional language teaching. A teacher's task is to explain how practices and purposes are realised in texts through language choices. Planners nominate texts for students' close analysis in order to see how texts work to make meanings. Instruction in language use and choice is explicit. Students as newcomers to content areas of a curriculum need to understand the kinds of texts for participation in actual practices. The study of grammar is based on texts which realise particular social practices. The grammar is studied as a system of lexico-grammatical choices for conveying meaning – meaning which in turn is interpreted by readers and listeners.

Assist Learners' Composing and Conversing

Students need experiences with numerous texts to gain familiarity with the purposes, practices and discourse features of texts. With access to examples of texts they observe what is a typical generic form of a text and how a text works for the expression of meanings. They draw upon the content of texts for discussion, for action and for composing texts. What is essential is experience of the specific semiotic resources which demarcate a field of human endeavour or area of action, whether it is the work of technicians, of practitioners, of professionals, of tradespeople, of artisans or of artists. In each case newcomers face challenges in participating in the special and defining practices of communities. In education there is deliberate instruction in discourses and in modelling community practices. Workplace and subject-specific programmes are based on the predictability of at least some of the practices which characterise subject knowledge and skills and therefore the discourses which enable those practices.

Planning programmes of work has become increasingly complex, with changes in programme goals from teaching grammar to learning to communicate. In traditional, grammar-based programmes it was easy for designers and teachers to prepare programmes: list grammar items, write exercises to practise them and select a reading text to illustrate the grammar and insert new vocabulary items. Teachers' preparation and instruction pri-oritised presenting and marking or correcting exercises. Teaching method, classroom activities and assessment were implicit in the design. But grammar rules, grammatical analysis and lexical choice were disconnected from practices and not easily linked to students' prior experiences and future action. In contrast, a programme based on social theory integrates analysis with resources for working together. A teacher can define aims and objectives which take account of community and epistemology, of teacher and student preferences and interests, of the availability and suitability of resources, and of the physical conditions for teaching. The selection of texts offers choice, so students observe variability of texts, and notice obligatory and optional elements in the discourse. In the next chapter I set out some practical strategies for instruction.

Summary

In planning a curriculum, teachers have opportunities to create programmes of interest to them and to their students. The freedom to craft a curriculum depends on school, system and assessment prescriptions. Planning requires the selection of texts that will allow active participation in the practices of a target community. The texts are the resources for participation and a focus for analysis of structure and wording, raising students' consciousness of grammatical features typical of text types.

Notes and Readings

Beginners are never really beginners. Children and adults in language programmes know a lot about making meaning with language. Some colleagues argue that beginners need basic grammatical knowledge and vocabulary before they can cope with texts. In this chapter I have suggested that we need to find out how to incorporate beginning learners' wide experiences of practices and texts in programme design. This is a topic for research in different contexts and for different languages.

I have suggested that social theory explains the success of teaching language through subject-specific or content-based programmes. De Zarobe and Catalan (2009) have published a very useful book on content teaching. I have argued for the value of content teaching in a study of science and home economics teaching (Mickan, 2007). The problem is that language instructors may not have expertise as engineers or historians or biologists in order to provide expert apprenticeship in subject-specific discourses. A proposal is to investigate the use of subject-specific corpora with concordancing programs (Adams, 2006) to begin to identify some of the discourse features of disciplines. The task is to collect subject-specific texts for inclusion in a corpus and to use these for analysis.

Tasks

(1) Nominate a target community and use the framework below to identify some of the defining practices and potential texts:

Target community	Practices for focus	Representative or potential texts
Sports training programme		
Science class		
Meditation class		
Chess club		
Accountancy office		

(2) Prior experiences. Plan a procedure for determining students' familiarity with practices and discourses specific to the goals of a program; ask students to identify text types and associated practices to help with programming.

(3) Subject-specific programme. Plan a curriculum outline for a subject-specific or content-based programme.

(4) Bilingual programmes. Document a bilingual programme by recording the subject-specific practices and discourses in the programme.

(5) Sequencing of texts. Discuss with your colleagues parameters for sequencing texts. What are priority practices? What features of texts do students know already? What text types are new to students? The selection of texts should take into account length of texts, selection of lexico-grammar (e.g. clause selection), and technical and abstract terminology, for the representation of meanings with increasing clarity, specificity and technicality.

6 Teaching Practices

the process we are interested in is that of producing and
understanding text in some context of situation....
Halliday and Hasan (1985: 14)

Introduction

In educational programmes socialisation is achieved to a considerable degree with language: teachers and students work together with spoken and written texts, teachers scaffold (or model – see below) learners' engagements with texts, and teachers and students together analyse discursive practices. Students learn by construing and sharing new meanings in texts – through working to understand and produce texts, through enjoyment of texts, through confrontations with ideas in texts, through critical analysis of the lexico-grammar of texts. The purpose of this chapter is to provide an overview of instruction as a process of socialisation of students into community practices and texts.

In Chapter 4 I outlined a framework for instruction which foregrounds students' making meanings as they work with texts (see Figure 4.4, p. 54). The aim of teaching activities is for students to experience, observe, analyse and formulate meanings with language as part of class members' practices. The focused and selective participation in and analysis of practices prepare students for the expression of their own meanings with language and with other semiotic tools. When instruction is directed to discourse, then understanding the meaning of texts and expressing meaning in texts is central to teaching.

Guiding Ideas

Social practice pedagogy has seven defining characteristics (Table 6.1). The focus of instruction is the teacher's deliberate selection of activities for students' comprehension and expression of meanings. A class community creates contexts for learning with texts through:

Table 6.1 Social practice pedagogy (adapted from Mickan, 2006: 15)

Characteristic	Features/examples
1. Community	People live in communities and interact and relate with semiotic resources – linguistic, material, spatial and physical– and with other symbolic and artistic mediums and tools
2. Membership	A teacher's goal is the development of learners' semiotic resources, that is, skills and knowledge, to participate in communities, at first as apprentices on the periphery of group, and over time developing into core, expert members
3. Socialisation	Teachers create social space in order to immerse learners selectively and progressively in the practices and meanings of chosen communities; in language education, attention is on the texts for social participation
4. Apprenticeship	Teachers plan and structure instruction to guide and to assist learners' pathways to participation through planned engagements in specific practices with texts
5. Analysis	Teachers and learners analyse the grammar of texts in order to make explicit discourse differences for the realisation of different social purposes and meanings
6. Participation	Teachers evaluate learners' knowledge and skills for membership, as demonstrated in their participation in community practices
7. Transformation	Community practices and discourses change with new membership and through contestation of existing practices; transformation occurs in response to cultural and environmental change, such as technological innovation

- immersion and participation in language-mediated events;
- observation of texts in contexts of use for authentic purposes;
- analysis of the role of language in mediating actions;
- attention to and awareness of the specific ways text structure and language selections realise different meanings for different practices;
- comprehension and formulation of meanings in regular and repeated speech and literacy events.

Teaching centres on learners' observations of texts functioning in practice, on creating opportunities for learners' experiences in the creation of meanings and on analysis of lexico-grammatical resources for the expression of meanings. The goal of classroom activities is students' task participation using the semiotic potential of the language system. Teachers select practices and texts for focused instruction and analysis of texts as preparation for students' personal and public expression of meanings. Learners as apprentices develop their skills in text interpretation and text formulation through language use.

Figure 6.1 Instructional procedures

The following assumptions guide the apprenticeship of learners into new community practices and discourses:

(1) People develop relationships, roles, skills and knowledge by taking part in the practices of multiple communities; they acquire capacities to choose and use semiotic resources for community participation through observation, action and the support of others.

(2) Experienced members support newcomers' or learners' use of resources in order to take part in community practices. Scaffolding (Gibbons, 2006) is a metaphor used to describe such assistance which experienced members provide to help learners with their new tasks. It describes the cooperative building of discourses for participation – the building of new meanings mediated through interactions with experienced others.

(3) Learners have opportunities for formulating, sharing and negotiating meanings with language for joint action, for the exchange of ideas, for the expression of feelings, for the development of concepts, for sharing experiences and for building relationships with people.

Teachers assist learners' participation through planned practices, as illustrated in Figure 6.1. Instruction begins with texts and content with which learners are familiar so that they can use their discourse and world knowledge for the prediction of meanings and for learning patterns of language in use. To enhance recognition and understanding, teachers choose texts with familiar topics, with illustrations and with recognisable design and layout. The introduction of new knowledge in unfamiliar texts needs initial guidance, but people are adept at working out and understanding new information in new formats.

Immersion in Text-Rich Practices and Modelling Texts of Social Practices

Instruction in schools, colleges or universities is generally discourse dependent and students' apprenticeship takes place to a large extent through language-based tasks. Lessons are spaces for semiotic activity. During lessons, teachers and students take part in activities designed to develop students' abilities for participation in planned practices. The orientation of activities is towards meaning-making – working with selections of texts, analysing characteristic discourse features of texts and their lexico-grammar, and composing texts.

Lessons are special times for teachers to model practices and for students to observe language in action. Students join a class as relative newcomers to a community in order to learn new practices under the guidance of a skilled teacher. Through many exchanges with teachers and peers, students develop discourses for taking part in class events, for doing set tasks and for working with peers. Through spoken and written interactions in lessons students learn the practices and discourses of curriculum subjects. They draw upon a wealth of previous discourse experiences in the interactions. The joint actions of teachers and students create opportunities for learners to construct meanings and develop skills for participation in lesson activities. There follow eight 'proposals' for instruction as a guide to teaching.

Proposal 1: Practices and texts

What makes the application of social theory to language teaching distinctive is the centrality of student contact with and analysis of texts – looking at, listening to, reading and talking about texts. A whole-text focus is embedded in practices which foreground people's language choices. Language and practices are mutually constitutive. Language is one of the sign systems for making sense of, and for taking part in, community. Text types or genres characterise particular practices. Teaching centres on the development of the lexico-grammatical resources of texts as meaning potential rather than on demonstrating grammatical features in isolation from social contexts. At the sight or sound of appropriately selected sample texts, students distinguish their linguistic features and visual images and formats, which trigger recognition of contexts and purposes of texts.

Proposal 2: Students' knowledge of practices and potential texts

The selection of texts should recognise students' prior socialisation experiences and their extensive familiarity with discourse practices. Planning a programme based on students' previous experiences creates a substantial bridge into a new subject area in a new class. For example, newcomers to a second-language programme are familiar with many text types and with the practices in which texts are embedded. They recognise features of many texts such as their generic structure and patterns. They know the roles of language in daily life so that their acquaintance with many texts is a way into teaching. As the purpose of class activities is to extend learners' semiotic capacities, teachers identify significant texts and other resources familiar to learners and relate them to the textual resources of the communities they are preparing to enter, and to enhance specialist skills in chosen communities for advanced learners.

Teachers begin instruction with practices and text types and content with which learners are familiar, so that they use their discourse and world knowledge for the prediction of meanings in patterns of language use. Students work with familiar texts with recognisable layouts and spatial designs (such as lists, advertisements, procedures), and topics, with accompanying illustrations.

Proposal 3: Students' experiences of speech events and literate practices

Teachers' and students' spoken and written texts in lessons are a vital source of students' experiences of working with language. The teacher has a central role in socialising learners into working with language. Classes are potentially rich in natural uses of oral and written language. Class members speak and read and write to manage events, tasks and relationships. The ecology of a class shapes the nature of discourse and the discourse shapes the activities of the class. It sets the scene for who will speak and how they will speak together. The teacher's talk is the source of students' observation of speech in action. Learners observe talk and action linked to routine practices. The teacher's reading and writing and talking about texts exemplify literate practices. Learners' need to do things with language in lessons – to carry out instructions, to maintain relationships, to participate in specified behaviours and routines – aids understanding and skill development through multiple, authentic class encounters.

On contact with texts we want to make sense of them – this applies to students' listening to the talk of teachers and fellow students as well as to written texts. Learners observe teachers as texts in action. Teachers model language use as texts for getting things done in lesson routines: discourses for class management, for giving instructions, for demonstrations and explanations of subject content, for disputation and appraisal, and for developing personal relationships. Teachers as speakers, readers and writers model and scaffold formulation of meanings for specific purposes. They choose texts for class members' realisation of selected social purposes. Immersed in text-rich environments with access to multiple and multimodal texts, students experience the semiotic functions of language in action as they talk, read, argue and compose together. They enjoy understanding and expressing meanings in the comprehension and composition of texts.

Proposal 4: Selection and preparation of practices and texts

As we participate in many different practices on a daily basis, our students need knowledge of many different text types. The selection of texts is determined by the particular social practices we want students to join in. These social practices are based on the community discourses which students are preparing to join or to develop expertise in, and are used, for example, to prepare students for joining a particular disciplinary area, such as biology or geography. The aim is to target those texts directly related to the aims of the course and the level of learners' proficiency or expertise. Instruction requires systematic planning to broaden learners' experiences and awareness of text types. A wide selection of texts includes topical and newsworthy texts and fun texts so that students become confident in using a range of text types – the idea is to develop the textualising skills of learners across a range of language practices. The selection of texts takes into consideration the following factors:

- they should be recognisable to learners;
- they should be relevant to learners;
- they should be real examples from the relevant community;
- they should be representative of community practices.

Proposal 5: Assisting expression of specific meanings

We experience texts as texture, that is, as patterns in performance of practices. The use of patterned texts or text types is part of learners' experiences. Learning new discourses requires conscious attention to the language features of text types which characterise specific practices. Learners need explicit knowledge about the formation of texts, about language features and patterns of text types. Teachers explain the social functions of text types and then work with students using many exemplars so that students become familiar with text conventions and they experience how particular text types are used in practice. Recognition of text type and its relationship to practice is what is significant. Students predict and infer meanings as they listen to or read texts and take notice of what is going on in a situation:

> In the normal course of life, all day and every day, when we are interacting with others through language, we are making these inferences … from the situation to the text, and from the text to the situation. (Halliday & Hasan, 1985: 36)

With reference to multiple examples of texts, students have material for their own analysis of variations in texts, of optional elements in texts and of intertextuality. The texts are also data for examination of lexico-grammatical choices made for specific purposes. With exemplars for reference, students build up textual resources for expression of their own meanings.

Proposal 6: Explaining lexico-grammatical selections and meanings

Teachers model texts to extend learners' own discourse resources. The strategy is for teachers to demonstrate the composing of texts so learners notice features which construe specific experiences. Students' observation of language in action sets contexts for making sense of what is happening with language. When learners are familiar with what is going on – recognition and understanding – they are ready to attend to the lexico-grammatical choices for conversing and composing. Instruction is directed to students' understanding of the role of language in what is happening. For Rothery (1996: 120), 'explicitness about how language works to mean, is at the heart of educational linguistics'. Text-focused activity highlights grammar in order to expose the lexical composition of texts and the patterns of language which enable listeners and readers to draw upon their knowledge and experiences of discourse patterns in predicting content and in dissecting and differentiating meanings.

Learners need instruction in how selected but significant features characterise text types. Analysis begins with examination of the wordings of the schematic structure characterising a text – how sections sequence,

---

Box 6.1 Recipe for *Kaeng Chud*, by Kamon and Chenchira

The following procedural text was written by teachers from Satun in Thailand.

Ingredients
200g shrimps
300g cabbage cut into 3 cm strips
2 tbsp chopped garlic
3 tbsp oil
1 tbsp fish sauce
4 cups water
1 tbsp chopped coriander

Method
1. Heat oil in frying pan, add garlic and fry until golden
2. Heat 4 cups of water in a pot
3. Boil shrimps in water for 3 minutes
4. Add cabbage for 1 minute
5. Add salt and fish sauce
6. Serve topped with coriander and fried garlic

organise and shape a text. Learners examine in detail lexical and syntactic selections comprising a text. As the linguistic resources of texts are complex, instruction focuses on the main features of a text for the identification of the characteristic wording of a particular text type.

Teachers use exemplars of texts from text banks for students to refer to for the composition of their own texts. The text in Box 6.1 is recognisable in our culture as a recipe. The text is organised in a particular way – as a procedural text. It sets out a procedure or steps for the preparation and cooking of a particular dish. The generic structure of the text lists the ingredients and quantities first, then the method or the procedure for meal preparation. These are obligatory or conventional components of the genre. Implicit in the text are aspects of the practices which people follow when they cook, beginning with the purchase of ingredients together with measurements and amounts, followed by the actions in sequence for cooking.

The stages of the text are constructed with grammatical selections for a particular purpose, which differentiates the text from other texts. Their awareness and identification of the language of the text prepares students for comprehending the content, for cooking and for recording cooking procedures in recipes for others.

Proposal 7: Conversing and composing: Formulating meanings in texts

Students' opportunities for language use in action are embedded in instructional practices, in schooling and in training programmes. Students learn to express meanings from observation of people working together and sharing meanings. Work with texts foregrounds the active, creative role of using the language system, as students formulate ideas, talk to get things done and chat with friends. Texts provoke responses for enquiring, arguing or reminiscing. With texts we confer, contest, debate and deliberate. Through our talk around texts we share meanings and construct meanings.

Proposal 8: Assessment of participation in social practices

Assessment evaluates candidates' abilities to take part in targeted social practices through the use of language. An examination presupposes a community of practice, entry to which is determined by tests which assess the readiness of an entrant for accreditation in the community or, as is the case with tests which assess general proficiencies such as communicative competence, for accreditation in a variety of communities of practice. Assessment is based on evidence of participation as a member of a specified community. Rather than measure lexical and syntactical items or similar discrete items, assessment is based on the notion of participation in social practices through the use of language – learners demonstrate their ability to join in social practices with appropriate discourse resources.

Social theory informs assessment in a number of ways:

(1) assessment comprises multiple semiotic actions;
(2) tests assess abilities to carry out specific social practices;
(3) the validity of tests rests on the relationship of task and discourse speci-fication to the social practices for which a candidate is taking the test.

Whereas in traditional assessment examiners identify errors and accuracy, in text-based assessment examiners focus on purpose and content, as conveyed in preferred texts for participation in community practices. General assessment procedures are listed in Box 6.2.

At the specific level of assessment tasks, the first question is, what are the social practices learners will engage in? The identification of practices enables the specification of discourses for candidates to display in a test, thus giving the test validity through the alignment of the purposes of the test and test outcomes. Test designers will therefore need to discriminate between texts and their purposes. The mark of participation in literacy practices and speech events is making the choices from the language system for the expression of appropriate meanings.

Two things need to be said about general-purpose and specific-purpose tests. A general-purpose test covers different communities and a multitude of practices realised with different semiotic resources. International testing systems (IELTS, TOEFL) are examples of this type. The validity of such test rests on the transfer of assessed skills or competencies across communities with their distinguishing practices. A curriculum for this kind of test identi-fies practices and semiotic resources which appear to apply in a general way

---

Box 6.2 General assessment procedures

- Identification of community or communities
- Listing of social practices
- Selection of key texts for realising social practices
- Specification of content referenced to texts
- Specification of obligatory discourse features characteristic of texts used to determine content criteria for assessment

to a community. This is the case with language proficiency tests designed as university entry tests. However, it is not possible to specify accurately the kinds of discourses necessary for entry to a specific community of practice. In contrast to a general-purpose test, a specific-purpose test – one designed, for example, to measure computing skills – prescribes community, practices and skills in the management of semiotic resources. This is the case with discipline-specific testing and assessment tasks, in which students are required to document observations, write literature reviews, submit reports or present critical analyses.

Testing usually requires management of multiple texts and modes. In examinations and for assessment tasks, learners undertake a series of discourse activities which require understanding and composition of different text types. Successful negotiation of a test involves a series of 'literacy events', which may include the following:

- *Comprehension of instructions.* The initial encounter involves understanding the instructions for the test, such as time allocation, number of tasks and maximum word count.
- *Interpretation of prompts.* Test takers need to interpret instructions related to the purpose of the test. They need to understand the prompt or question and to determine the nature of the response – what is expected in the task. For example, in a test which requires written responses the task needs to specify the practice(s) which are meant to be fulfilled. A typical example is writing an essay. But an essay is a general text type which needs to be qualified at more specific levels as an exposition, an argument text or a discussion text (Mickan, 2003). A prompt suggests a particular social response and candidates need to predict what text type is expected for the appropriate exchange of meanings with the examiner.
- *Selection of text types and wordings appropriate to task realisation.* In language-mediated activities, assessment is based on discourse selections appropriate to the realisation of practices and to assessors' social expectations. The prompt directs candidates towards the use of particular discourses. Candidates need to select the discourse resources to respond appropriately to the specific expectations of a test question or section. Examiners or markers of tests have expectations of text types: they require text-based specifications for their evaluation of a candidate's texts.

Summary

The teaching approach outlined in this chapter applies to general and to language-mediated instruction. It emphasises learners' work with texts in repeated and purposeful speech and literacy encounters. It requires the deliberate analysis of texts, targeting selected features typical of a genre or text type. The analysis of text structure and wording draws learners' attention to the function of the text and the social practices realised with the text.

Notes and Readings

The term 'community' is used here to describe people working together towards a shared goal or goals. In education, teachers and students come together in the roles of instructors and learners with the specific purpose of apprenticeship – of learning from teachers who are insiders in terms of their knowledge; they learn together with others who are, more or less, on the periphery of the community of speakers, readers and writers.

The prominence given to social practices is for two key reasons: firstly, to clarify the purpose of an activity – what this instructional activity will enable a student to do; and secondly, to deal with the criticism that schooling activities are not 'real world' and therefore that the language taught is not ex-perienced authentically in lessons. The practices in schools are representative of practices in society and the discourses learned to perform sets of practices provide the foundation for learning how to participate in new practices.

Scholars who have studied and taught languages following traditional methods are sceptical of teaching with texts, particularly with learners in the early stages of instruction. One of my postgraduate students teaching English as a second language to a class of overseas adult students with basic literacy skills decided to risk teaching with whole texts to her students, rather than working through the grammar-based texts recommended for the course. She prepared written texts with photographs about her family. She was surprised with the results – students related to the pictures and texts about her family, they understood her extended presentation, and they wrote about their own families. Even students peripherally involved took part. Her experiences and those of others suggest that teachers could begin by undertaking small-scale investigations into text-based teaching and record and analyse the results.

Teaching with texts influences the choice of topics or themes handled in class. Language teaching in beginning and in general classes for a long time dealt with a narrow range of topics – family, leisure activities, greetings, seasons, holidays, travel, festivals. Topics were unrelated to learners' interests and they were artificial exercises in mouthing opinions and dialogues. With the application of social theory to the determination of content, the selection of themes and texts is based on a community and its practices. In class, teachers are readers and writers as well as interlocutors and they choose topics and texts of real interest to them as well as to their students.

Tasks

(1) Hyland (2004a: 132) describes texts as 'the interactions of people who are members of specific communities'. Identify a community and determine through observation or survey the texts which community members use for doing things together.

(2) A narrative is a popular text type, which has a recognisable generic structure. The following short narrative, entitled 'The Greedy Dog', was produced by Kamon and Chenchira at a workshop in Satun, Thailand in 2002:

> Once upon a time there was a dog. It was very hungry, so it went to the market and stole some beef and ran away. It walked over a bridge, and saw the reflection of the beef in the water. It looked bigger than the real beef. The dog said to itself, 'the beef in the water is bigger than my beef!' So the dog dropped the beef in the river. Suddenly, the beef disappeared. The dog was very sad. It sat on the bridge and cried because it was very hungry. It was a foolish dog.
>
> Moral: The greedy lose all.

Analyse the structure of the text – the stages of the narrative – and the wording or lexico-grammatical choices which determine the progression of the narrative. What discourse features would you identify for explicit teaching?

(3) Okawa (2008) documented the literacy practices and texts a nursing student encountered in different literacy events. One series of events he observed were lectures, during which he took field notes and made an audio-recording. The following table summarises the student's practices connected with a lecture.

Literacy events	Literacy practices	Texts
Before the lecture	• Reading the study plan • Reading textbooks about nursing diagnoses and the musculoskeletal system	• Printed study plan • Printed textbooks (text types = explanation and diagrams)
During the lecture	• Listening to the lecturer talk about nursing problem-solving and nursing nomenclature • Taking notes • Using an electronic dictionary	• PowerPoint presentation • Information on white board: vocabulary; diagram • Student's lecture notes
After the lecture	• Watching a video stream	• Displayed electronic text • Lecture displayed in electronic mode • Lecture notes written by student

Observe a lesson, lecture or similar literacy event and document the social practices and texts which a student needs to manage to take part in the event. Interview or talk with a student about the preparation and follow-up associated with the event. Summarise the information in a table.

(4) Observe a lesson and document the social practices in the class. What texts and what resources do students need to learn to participate in these community (social) practices?

(5) Prepare a teaching plan which incorporates some text-based activities for a programme in which grammatical tests determine most or all of the content.

7   Curriculum Applications

Introduction

The curriculum design outlined in this book is adaptable to learners' interests and aspirations across age groups, programmes and institutions. The purpose of this chapter is to illustrate the application of social theory to the design of curricula in different contexts. The selected examples primarily use texts as units of analysis for curriculum design.

Foreign-Language and Second-Language Programmes

Languages are taught in diverse circumstances, from schools with nationally accredited programmes to locally organised cram schools and pre-school playgroups. The theory of learning which underpins the design of curricula described in previous chapters is applicable to formal and to informal programmes in foreign-language and in second-language settings. My students often argue that teaching in foreign-language settings, where the target language is not used in the community in which it is taught, is different from teaching in second-language contexts, where the language is used in the community. They argue that grammar-based teaching is suitable for foreign-language contexts rather than teaching for communication. This is true where the purpose of a language programme is linguistic analysis – the study of the grammar of a language. If, on the other hand, the purpose of a programme is the development of communication skills, then students need opportunities for communication, which can take place in foreign-language lessons as well as in second-language classes. Conditions for learning to make meanings with language are comparable in both settings. In both contexts learning is a social semiotic activity – learning to understand and express meanings with language. Teaching practices based around texts create conditions for communication and texts are significant resources for communication.

The language ecologies in English as a second language (ESL) and English as a foreign language (EFL) are definitely different, so adaptation to the eco-social conditions in foreign-language classes is necessary. Many factors influence the teaching environment – teachers' experiences, national and school policies, programme purposes, students' expectations, access to target-language speakers, as well as to electronic and other texts. In ESL environments learners have the opportunity to talk and read in a target language on a daily basis outside the classroom. ESL programmes in South Australia are of this kind. In EFL contexts, making meaning in the target language occurs primarily if not exclusively in lessons, and there are few opportunities for speaking English face-to-face outside of lessons. For the EFL teacher the responsibility to create lessons rich in semiotic activities is therefore vital. Lessons are ideal events for target-language communication because a common purpose for a language class is using language as a signifier in that community. The examples in this chapter apply social theory to curriculum designs in different contexts.

Secondary-School German: A Foreign-Language Programme

This programme was one of my early experiences in working with texts for teaching high-school students in a foreign-language programme. The texts were specially selected for local students in a regional high school in South Australia. The context of the programme was a former technical high school in Port Pirie, an industrial city built around a large lead smelter. When I was appointed to the school, the German programme used grammar-based textbooks and audio-visual materials with artificial exercises and dialogues, which students found boring and which did not help us to work together in German. The new communicative courses were not much better. A newly purchased communicative textbook used in French classes was published in the United Kingdom and written for Scottish children planning a trip to France. The dialogues, situations and pictures were unrelated to the lives of children in a regional Australian industrial city, where students did not envisage visiting France, let alone travelling there via Scotland.

The problem was to find a textbook relevant to students' lives in Port Pirie. Instead of purchasing a commercial textbook, local teachers of German and I wrote a resource book of texts on topics specially selected for our students. We chose texts for students to be able to communicate about their lives, interests and experiences with one another and with pen-friends in Germany. The practical purpose of the texts was to exchange experiences in German with similarly aged students in Germany. This was a decade before emails so we used our personal contacts in Germany to exchange letters with German pen-pals and teachers. Topics and teenager magazine articles and letter texts supported our use of German for working together in lessons. Students had lots of text-based work, including working with exemplars of texts in a locally printed resource book. The resources comprised speaking German together in class, a library with German books for independent reading, personal journal entries based on modelled texts in the resource book, German magazines written for foreign learners, and letters and articles from pen-pals. We used German to learn about contemporary life in Germany. At the same time, the students studied the vocabulary and grammar of authentic texts, not as abstract items but to record events, and to relate and appraise experiences. Students had a purpose for learning German – to share ideas and experiences with their pen-pals.

Teaching with selected texts reduced my stress in class as students were not repeating meaningless expressions and dialogues or doing exercises on decontextualised grammar. They were able to work with some independence, self-selecting and reviewing books, writing journal entries, reading letters from German pen-pals and responding to them, and finding out about the lives of their age group in Germany. We enjoyed working with texts – reading aloud, discussing topics, receiving letters from Germany and sharing the contents. The energising effect of learners engaging in literacy tasks with authentic texts – actual audiences and real purposes – showed me the potential for dynamic work with texts, including for beginners.

Bilingual Italian Programme

The next example comes from a year-long evaluation I directed of a bilingual Italian programme (Mickan, 2006). Bilingual programmes are designed to teach subject content or disciplinary knowledge and skills in a selected language. The Italian programme was introduced to a class of 15 children in their first year of schooling in a South Australian primary school. Only two of the children were of Italian background, so the programme was designed for English-speaking children. The programme was based on the state-approved curriculum for teaching grade 1 children in primary schools. Prior to commencement of the programme, the teacher was supported by the school and a consultant to develop resources in Italian for teaching the subjects health, religion, society and environment, and science. The school timetable allocated the second half of each school day to the Italian bilingual programme.

Lessons were held in a room designed and decorated for teaching Italian. The aims of the programme were to teach in Italian the content of the

Table 7.1 Timetable in the bilingual programme (Mickan, 2006: 347)

	Session 1 (before lunch)	Session 2 (after lunch)	Session 3 (after lunch)
Monday	Religion	Society and environment	Science
Tuesday	Religion	Health	Society and environment
Wednesday	Religion	Science	Society and environment
Thursday	Religion	Society and environment	Health
Friday	Religion	Science	Development/play

four selected subjects. Italian was the accepted medium of communication. When the children walked into the Italian classroom they formed an Italian-speaking community with the explicit purpose of conducting business in Italian, under the guidance of a native Italian speaker. As a process of socialisation, the children were newcomers, observing and listening to subject content spoken in Italian. Resources for teaching included the teacher modelling Italian use for working together and texts from the subjects taught in the curriculum (e.g. for religion – prayers; for health – diagrams with labels of the digestive tract; for society and environment – classification of Australian animals). The timetable (Table 7.1) integrated skills and linguistic topics. The themes the children studied were based on the subjects and topics and texts in the normal first-grade curriculum: the liturgy for worship, child development, healthy living, care for animals. Table 7.2 gives examples from term 3.

From the beginning of the programme, the teacher used Italian for class management, for giving instructions to children, for teaching subject content and for social purposes (Mickan, 2006). When the children came

Table 7.2 Subjects and themes for term 3 in the bilingual programme (Mickan, 2006: 347)

Subjects	Themes
Religion	Congregation day Paraliturgy
Society and environment	Growing and changing
Health	Food, energy and growth
Science	Animals need food, air and water Worm farms

for Italian lessons at midday, they entered a room equipped with Italian signs and pictures, with Italian texts, games and books. The children made a physical transition from an English-speaking to an Italian ecology. Here it was natural for the teacher to work with the children in Italian; she used gestures, illustrations and diagrams labelled in Italian and wall texts to support comprehension. Italian was embedded in children's work, immersing them in many different spoken and written texts of the subjects they were studying. The children followed instructions in Italian and carried out tasks in Italian.

The enthusiasm of young children working in Italian with the teacher was an instructive experience in the application of social theory. The children with their teacher formed an Italian community organised to apprentice children in practices which defined the subjects of health, religion, society and environment, and science in the school's curriculum. Teacher and children worked in Italian without the need to devise special tasks: activities stemmed from the content of the curriculum for each subject and defined practices and texts. Topics and tasks were age-related and linked to children's experiences and community: children studied the religion of the school community; they visited a mobile nature van with Australian animals (echidna, hopping mice, frogs). Although Italian was taught in a context which could be described as foreign, in lessons children experienced socialisation in Italian as a normal, everyday experience.

A Science Class: Content-Based Instruction for ESL Students

Comparable to a bilingual programme, content-based instruction means teaching a subject or subjects such as history, or chemistry or mathematics in a target language (De Zarobe & Catalan, 2009). Students' socialisation takes place through their participation in practices comprising the field of a subject. In a study of ESL teaching to migrant high school children in South Australia (Mickan, 2007), the children were taught ESL through the subjects of the curriculum such as science and home economics. In science, ESL students experienced language in use for taking part in science-related activities.

The aim of the science curriculum was to introduce students to elementary scientific practices using English. Within the community of the science class, lesson activities socialised students as apprentice scientists in a number of practical ways. The teacher's talk apprenticed students into the technical language and tasks of science. Students worked with scientific discourses in their spoken exchanges with the teacher, in reading texts and diagrams in the textbook, and in writing up experiments. In the science laboratory students followed instructions for conducting experiments. They talked together to do the experiments. They responded to the teachers' questions reflecting on the results of experiments. After practical laboratory lessons, students wrote up results of the experiments based on the characteristic text type of a science report.

Students were exposed to and used many text types. They experienced scientific discourses in spoken instructions, in diagrams, definitions and explanations, and in practical experiments in a science laboratory. The oral and written discourses and the diagrammatic representations of scientific procedures were authentic and normal. The teacher's talk, the textbook passages and diagrams, and the collaborative conversations with peers contributed to students' apprenticeship into a science community.

A Science Curriculum

The science curriculum at the Adelaide Secondary School of English illustrates a text-based curriculum for a school subject. An extract from the *Pathway: A Science Curriculum* (Adelaide Secondary School of English, 2006) illustrates the framework for the science programme. Pathway A was designed for students without previous education in English.

The tabulated topic overview (see Box 7.1, which presents a summary of the overview) sets out a sequence for teaching science over two years. The curriculum is organised around science-related topics and teaching objectives, which imply discourses for doing science. The discourses are contextualised in the typical social practices of science (Mickan, 2006) designed as a programme of apprenticeship for participation in the activities of scientists.

Similarly, the curriculum sets out detailed tabulated teaching directions for each topic. 'Animals' (see Box 7.2) was the introductory topic for instruction. The plan names 'Key Ideas and Science Skills', which distinguish specific scientific practices such as observation and identification ('Recognise and identify Australian animals'), defining phenomena ('Define vertebrates and invertebrates'), and classification ('Classify vertebrates...'). At this stage of the programme, the genre identified as a focus is 'Label diagrams', although students will be exposed to other genres of science at the same time. The plan analyses language items for development based on systemic functional grammar. The lexico-grammatical details presuppose teachers' familiarity with the grammar for application to specific practices, although examples are given for each grammatical item. The curriculum is a map for teachers planning lessons to apprentice students as scientists.

Box 7.1 Science curriculum pathway A at the Adelaide Secondary School of English: Topic overview

Foundation (two terms)
Animals
- Name and identify characteristics of common animals with emphasis on Australian animals
- Define and distinguish between vertebrates and invertebrates

Laboratory skills: apparatus
- Recognise apparatus
- Identify the materials from which apparatus is made of
- Identify the uses of apparatus

Plants
- Identify and classify plants as flowering or non-flowering plants
- Understand the functions of the different parts of the flowering plants
- Identify products and uses of plants
- Draw and label diagrams

Laboratory skills: using apparatus
- Understand safety requirements in the laboratory
- Understand different aspects of Bunsen burner (parts, lighting, heating)
- Understand the process of simple experiments (how to use common apparatus for experimentation; handling liquids; handling solids; heating solids; evaporating; filtering)

Intermediate (two terms)
Astronomy
- Understand the meaning of stars and constellations
- Discuss our closest star (i.e. the sun)
- Discuss the nine planets in terms of their size, distance from the sun and their special features
- Understand the rotation and revolution of the Earth and how day, night and the seasons occur
- Understand the Earth's satellite (i.e. the moon)
- Demonstrate and discuss the phases of the moon
- Discuss the influence of astronomy and cosmology across cultures

Magnets
- Carry out experiments to understand the properties of magnets
- Discuss the use of magnets across cultures

Microscope/cell structure
- Identify parts of a microscope
- Learn how to use a microscope
- Understand the structure of animal and plant cells
- Prepare wet mount slides

Body systems
- Introduce the concept of cells forming tissues and tissues forming cells
- Discuss the organs of the human body
- Understand the circulatory system
- Understand the digestive system

OR

Energy for living things
- Understand photosynthesis
- Understand life cycles
- Understand food chains and webs
- Understand ecosystems and adaptations for living in ecosystems

Advanced (two terms) *(headings summary only presented here)*
- States of matter
- Physical and chemical changes
- Atomic structure, elements, compounds and mixtijres
- Writing a scientific experiment report

Transition (two terms) *(headings summary only presented here)*
- Choose four topics from:
- Acids, bases and indicators
- Heat
- Light
- Electricity
- Rocks and Earth history

Box 7.2 Example topic ('Animals', from the 'Life systems' strand) from the science curriculum pathway A at the Adelaide Secondary School of English

Key ideas and science skills
- Recognise and identify Australian animals
- Identify characteristics of Australian animals
- Recognise and identify animals in general
- Define vertebrates and invertebrates
- Distinguish between vertebrates and invertebrates
- Classify vertebrates as fish, reptiles, amphibians, mammals and birds
- Identify characteristics of animals in each group

Genre development in the topic
- Label diagrams

Language development in the topic
Genre
Reference items:
- personal pronouns (e.g. *I, it, they*)
- demonstrative pronouns (e.g. *This* is an emu)
- indefinite/definite articles (*a/an, the*)

Word sets:
- hyponymy (classification) (e.g. animals – *vertebrates, invertebrates, mammals*)
- myronymy (composition or part/whole relationship) (e.g. bird – *claws, feathers, beak*)

Conjunctions (e.g. *and, because, or*)
Relative pronouns (e.g. *which, whose, that*)

Field
Everyday vocabulary (e.g. *animals, tongue, body*)
Technical vocabulary (e.g. *vertebrate, invertebrate*)
Noun groups as participants (e.g. *a long tongue*)
- pointer: *a*
- describer: *long*
- thing: *tongue*

Processes:
- action (e.g. *fly, catch, eat*)
- relational (e.g. *am/is/are, has/have*)

Circumstances:
- place (e.g. *on the ground, in the water*)

Prepositions (e.g. *on, in, inside, near, from*)
Comparatives (e.g. *very tall*)

Tenor
Speech functions

Student activities
- Copy the names of the Australian animals
- Complete sentences
- Label diagrams of the Australian animals
- Complete crossword
- Match names of Australian animals to pictures
- Label characteristics of Australian animals
- Brainstorm sentences
- Tick the correct sentence
- Label diagrams of animals in general
- Pronounce the names of the different animals
- Read simple books and complete comprehension

Language and learning outcomes
- Name animals
- Recognise Australian animals
- Classify vertebrates
- Identify characteristics of fish, mammals, reptiles, amphibians and birds

Literacy – Genre Mapping Across the Curriculum

The next model was developed by consultants in a Catholic primary school. The curriculum is genre based with a focus on written text types. The curriculum is applied across all teaching areas identified in the official education department curriculum. The design is referred to as a map; it provides, in other words, a guide for planning, teaching and assessing. The introduction to the curriculum document states its purpose:

> Its aim is to provide a systematic approach to teaching language features of written genres, which students need to master in order to achieve the outcomes of the SACSA [South Australian Curriculum Standards and Accountability] Framework. This map is a valuable resource for the written component of our literacy programs. The document maps the language requirements as described in the SACSA Scope and Scales, therefore ensuring our ESL students have equal access to the curriculum.
>
> Each teacher must, at a minimum, comprehensively and explicitly teach the four genres listed for their year levels. Suggested teaching ideas and a grammar resource are included in this document. Assessment proformas are also included. (White & Custance, 2003)

A table (reproduced here as Table 7.3) summarises genres for focused instruction across the curriculum.

The curriculum identifies seven genres for explicit teaching: Description, Explanation, Exposition, Narrative, Procedure, Recount, Report. The selected genres are considered to be widely used in school programmes. The seven genres are introduced and consolidated progressively in a cyclical process, so learners engage with each genre repeatedly and with increasing elaboration. Genres are introduced for experience initially, but as the programme advances, the structure and wordings of genres are taught explicitly.

The programme includes assessment pro formas, and these are shown in Table 7.4. The framework sets up consistency across year levels and subjects, so that what one teacher does in one subject is picked up and developed in other subjects as well. Children build their language awareness through repeated exposure to genre features, so that they are able to make specific choices in composing texts.

With this curriculum, teachers map their programmes collaboratively as they use a common language and learning theory. Teachers develop with each other and with their children shared discourses and a common metalanguage for working together. The genre-based pedagogy is designed

Table 7.3 Overview of genres to be explicitly taught at each year level

	Reception	Year 1	Year 2	Year 3	Year 4	Year 5	Year 6	Year 7
Description	Teach	Teach	Consolidate	Consolidate	Consolidate	Consolidate	Consolidate	Consolidate
Explanation	Expose	Teach: sequential	Teach: sequential	Consolidate	Teach	Teach	Consolidate	Teach: causal
Exposition	Expose	Expose	Teach: argument	Teach: argument	Teach: argument	Teach: argument	Teach: discussion	Teach: discussion/ debate
Narrative	Expose	Teach	Teach	Consolidate	Teach	Teach	Teach	Consolidate
Procedure	Teach	Consolidate	Teach	Teach	Consolidate	Teach	Consolidate	Consolidate
Recount	Teach	Consolidate	Consolidate	Teach	Consolidate	Consolidate	Teach: biography	Teach: historical
Report	Teach	Teach	Consolidate	Teach	Teach	Consolidate	Teach: research	Teach: taxonomic

Table 7.4 Assessment pro forma for reception year children, for the genre 'Recount'

Name:	Reception: Recount		
	No evidence	Developing	Achieved
Orientation sequence of events, reorientation			
Organising conjunctions: First, next, then, after, last			
Pronouns: I, we, you			
Phrases of time: today, tomorrow, yesterday, Saturday			
Phrases of place: at school, at the shops.			
Responds to who, what, when, where questions appropriately			
Evaluative language to express feelings and attitudes			
Foregrounds Next, then, after			
Past tense			

Name:	Reception: Description		
	No evidence	Developing	Achieved
Introduction of subject, characteristic features of the subject			
Third person pronouns: it he she him her			
Numbers: eight, four or five			
Describers: pretty, cute			
Classifiers class room, lounge room			
Articles: a, an, the			
Auxiliaries: do, does, is, are, was			
Foregrounds topic words			
Present tense			

for the development of children's confident selection and use of language through lots of text-based experiences and through language awareness activities.

English Learning Area: Tasmania Department of Education (2010)

The next example is of an official state department curriculum which recognises the centrality of texts across the curriculum. The extracts below are taken from the 'Tasmanian Statement on English' from the Department of Education of the Australian state of Tasmania. The curriculum places texts as core components of the curriculum.

> The field of English is intimately concerned with language and imagination. English is about making meaning through interaction with and reflection on texts, language, people and the world.
>
> Developing proficiency in English enables students to become critical, imaginative and reflective thinkers, effective communicators and active, lifelong learners. By engaging with, analysing and composing a diverse range of texts, students develop increasing control over the cultural, social and technical dimensions of language. Today's English classroom reflects the changing nature, contexts and uses of texts in an increasingly globalised world.
>
> Text is any communication involving language and can be written, read, spoken, visual, aural, performance or multimodal. Language is a vehicle people use to receive, interpret, respond to and create texts.
> (Tasmania Department of Education, 2010a)

The curriculum statement describes texts in more detail.

- Texts can be spoken, written or visual. Although written text probably comes first to mind for most of us, a text is any communication, spoken, written or visual, involving language. When the word, 'text', is encountered in the English statement or profile, it is this broad range of texts that is intended. Students work with texts such as conversations, speeches, letters, novels, plays, feature films and multi-media texts.
- Some texts combine words and images or sound to make meaning. Ads, picture books, documentaries and world wide web pages are just a few examples. In an increasingly visual world, there are more and

more texts like this. Teachers are learning how to help their students to interpret and create all the different aspects of these texts. They recognise that being able to this is an essential literacy skill: Literacy … involves the integration of speaking, listening, viewing and critical thinking with reading and writing …. Teachers have often found it useful to start with static texts such as picture books and print ads.

- New types of texts make different demands on students. Hypertext documents and e-mail are good examples. These kinds of texts invite different ways of reading and writing. In e-mail, the language used is a kind of hybrid of speech and writing. The conventions used are different from either phone conversations or letters. Hypertext texts are different from most print texts because there isn't one clear linear direction. The skills required for students to make the most of these texts are different from the skills needed for other texts.

Which texts are used in the English programme?

- All learning areas use texts. What makes English a unique learning area is what students do with three particular kinds of texts – literature, mass media and everyday texts.

(Tasmania Department of Education, 2010b)

The curriculum demonstrates how texts permeate instruction. It identifies different texts and modalities – spoken and written language combined with images and sounds to represent meaning potential.

Curriculum Adaptation and Extension

An official curriculum, whether national or local, may offer opportunities for adaptation and extension to formal requirements to incorporate text-based activities. The two studies reported below concern EFL contexts in which an official programme was adapted and extended. The EFL programmes were in Korean schools – one in a normal secondary school and the other in an independent institute with EFL programmes for young learners.

National curriculum: Adaptation of an EFL programme in a middle secondary school

Lim (2006, 2007) studied the discourse in English lessons in a secondary school in South Korea. The Korean national curriculum recommends classes which are collaborative, task-based and learner-centred. An aim of the curriculum is the development of learners' natural expression in English. The curriculum is aimed at teaching students 'to comprehend and produce modern everyday English' (Lim, 2007: 65), with two key objectives: '1) to obtain interest and confidence in English and to develop basic communication skills; 2) to communicate naturally in English on everyday life and general topics' (Lim, 2007: 66).

For her study, Lim (2007) observed a class in which lessons were based on a standard textbook with recorded but invented dialogues. The dialogues lacked cohesion and coherence. In a series of intervention lessons, Lim (2006, 2007) adapted resources to fit with topics in the textbook. The aim was to introduce students to authentic texts. To illustrate a 'procedure' text, she used a text with instructions for making a seed germinator. She compared students' questions in lessons based on the textbook with intervention lessons. In the former, the discourse mostly consisted of word and sentence repetition and grammar explanations. When making the seed germinators, students asked questions about the meanings of words and instructions, and sometimes made comments about the task. Students were interested in the text – they wanted to make sense of it so that they could build their own seed germinators. From a social theory perspective, the procedure for making a seed germinator stimulated students' natural talk about the text – they wanted to know the meaning of the text. Procedure text types link language to social practices for making or doing things – in this case to assemble a seed germinator. Students accessed a text type familiar to them and with the example of the instructions for making a seed germinator, they had a practical purpose for understanding the lexico-grammar.

The study illustrated how even in circumstances with programmes set to prepare students for national examinations, teachers have options to select and adapt programmes with texts to meet national policy objectives and at the same time to work with authentic texts. Lim's (2007) use of authentic texts widened students' scope for making meanings. With everyday texts, students employed wordings congruent with communicative practices and with curriculum objectives.

Curriculum extension by reading

Kim (2006) conducted a study in a private franchised English institute in Korea with about 80 students. In the institute, teachers used set course books as curriculum guides. The books contained invented reading passages and grammatical exercises. The readings were not written for reading for interest, but to illustrate grammatical usage and to do practice comprehension and translation exercises. Kim introduced an extensive reading programme. This was run as an adjunct to the main programme and within the constraints of a private school's program. According to Kim (2006: 27):

> *Extensive Reading* is a good way to incorporate text-based teaching. In other words, by introducing *Extensive Reading* principles we can utilise different types of texts such as multimedia or written text, and text-types such as informational, narrative or procedural texts for classroom activities.

Kim set up the extensive reading class with more than 100 English books purchased for a class library. He chose the books after observing local children browsing for books in an Adelaide bookshop; after talking with children about their book preferences; and after monitoring read-aloud segments in children's television shows. His book selection criteria included: a variety of text types, students' gender, place of publication, cultural characteristics of different authors, level of reading difficulty, and thickness of books. His purpose was to stimulate young (12–14-year-old) students' interest in free reading. A meeting was held with parents to explain the purposes and benefits of an extensive reading programme.

The books were displayed for children to see and they were able to select their own reading; the children read at their own pace and kept a record of their reading. By reading different texts, children engaged directly with varied meanings of language use beyond the word and sentence level. Kim (2006) monitored the children and found their amount of reading increased. Prior to the programme, five students had read an average of 1.8 books in English. At the end of the extensive reading programme, they had read an average of 39.2 books and they had positive attitudes towards reading. Students claimed that extensive reading helped their writing skills and all students claimed that reading improved their speaking proficiency. Kim (2006: 38) found that 'In only ten weeks students started to read English books for pleasure and discovered that reading is not only fun but also supports their language acquisition'. He commented that in large classes extensive reading allowed students to work and read at their own level. He concluded that 'Many meaningful texts helped students to develop English skills in literacy, not with pressure but pleasure' (Kim, 2006: 38).

An extensive reading programme is a practical application of social theory to language instruction. Through reading for interest, enjoyment, action and information, learners gain understandings of texts and of lexico-grammar which they use for action, in discussions and in composing texts themselves. Texts are normal starting points for action and discussion. Learners select expressions from what they hear and read for taking part in discussions, explanations and arguments. What distinguishes extended reading programmes from traditional reading for comprehension is self-management of reading: choice of reading matter, purposeful reading for pleasure, action and information, and all the time reading for meaning. Reading socialises learners into literacy practices, exposing them to text resources for self-expression and participation in community practices.

Language Revival: Example of an Australian Aboriginal Language – Ngarrindjeri

This model outlines the application of social theory to the language revival of a South Australian Aboriginal language. Considerable documentation of the language in the 19th century included word lists and expressions, and religious and other texts. Some expressions continue to be used in the community. The purpose of the project was to train Ngarrindjeri community members to use their language in the community, and for teaching in school programmes (Gale & Mickan, 2008). The focus was on the class as a community, relearning Ngarrindjeri for community use and for teaching in local schools. Elders and community members were enthusiastic about extending the use of Ngarrindjeri beyond a variety of expressions embedded in English syntax. The goal was for class members to use Ngarrindjeri for everyday practices, thus restoring language into community use as discourses or texts. The methodological aim was to use Ngarrindjeri in class work, for community applications and for teaching in school programmes. The class included elders, teachers, administrators and community members. The programme integrated language analysis – how the grammar worked – with the composition of texts. It was based on Ngarrindjeri people's wish to use the language in their daily lives.

The programme was framed around a number of concepts:

- Ngarrindjeri is a resource for making meanings (social semiotic).
- Ngarrindjeri is part of people's cultural practices – situated in country.
- Texts are embedded in people's practices – what human beings do together.
- Learning Ngarrindjeri is a process of socialisation – using Ngarrindjeri for the expression of meanings in relationships, in doing things together and in teaching.
- Texts are units of analysis for the design of teaching materials as they display language in use.
- Teachers need knowledge of the lexico-grammar in order to analyse texts for composing and teaching.

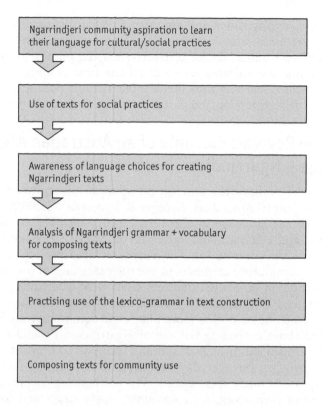

Figure 7.1 Teaching Ngarrindjeri in the context of social practices

---

Box 7.3 Texts and social practices developed in the Ngarrindjeri programme

- Official welcome to Ngarrindjeri land
- Greetings – personal and community
- Personal expressions of affection – in poetry
- Hymns and songs for community singing
- Descriptions of places and things
- Composing skits and games
- Recounting past experiences
- Preparing texts for teaching components of the early childhood curriculum, integrated into maths, health and language studies
- Football slogans
- Laments for funerals

Teaching was carried out using the pedagogic framework shown in Figure 7.1.

In workshops, participants were introduced to language resources and to language analysis. Within a couple of lessons an elder, Auntie Eileen, had written a *Welcome to Land Speech* and used it in reconciliation meetings and at other community events. Over a series of workshops participants created a variety of Ngarrindjeri texts for use with community members (Box 7.3).

On completion of the first stage of the programme, the class community celebrated with a graduation ceremony and sang a graduation-day song composed for the ceremony. The Ngarrindjeri people extended language use beyond the study of archival texts into community practices. The project is ongoing, as language restoration involves community in a long journey.

English as a Second-Language Curriculum for Schools

The Department of Education, Training and Employment (2005) in South Australia used a comprehensive text-based framework for programming the teaching of English as a second language (ESL) in primary and secondary schools. The curriculum ('ESL Scope and Scales') is based on systemic functional grammar. The content of the ESL curriculum is taught through spoken, written and multimodal texts. The curriculum combines instruction in texts with analysis of language, as summarised in Table 7.5. The social purposes of texts are made explicit, as indicated in Table 7.6.

Teachers use the curriculum for the identification of genres and for explaining the purposes of texts. The interesting point is that working with texts normally takes place with overlapping and interwoven genres as different purposes are pursued. The intertextuality of social discourse naturally envelops learners in language experiences beyond instruction in a particular genre. The curriculum is an advanced application of systemic functional linguistics applied to language teaching on a wide scale, at different levels of schooling, with success.

Table 7.5 Context and language for the 'ESL Scope and Scales' curriculum

Sociocultural context	Text in context	Language
Genre	Describes the range of text types, or genres, their specific purposes, their structure and their cohesion	Describes the language choices that structure texts appropriately and make them cohesive

Table 7.6 Genres and purposes, adapted from the 'ESL Scope and Scales' curriculum

	Genre	Purpose
Story genres	Narrative and traditional stories such as fables, myths	To entertain as well as to instruct the reader or listener about cultural values
	Personal recount	To record chronologically a series of past personal events in order to entertain, and to form and build on relationships
Factual genres	Description	To describe some of the features of particular people, places or things...
	Information report taxonomic descriptive	To provide accurate and relevant information about our living and non-living world. Reports often include visual texts. A taxonomic report will usually answer the question 'What kinds?', while a descriptive report will answer 'What about?' (e.g. a report entitled 'Whales' will usually be taxonomic, while one entitled 'The Humpback Whale' will be descriptive)
	Practical report	To provide a recount of the method undertaken in a practical, as well as the results and the conclusions
	Recount biographical historical	To relate chronologically a series of past events in order to inform. These events may concern an individual other than the writer (biographical recounts); or may be about events that occurred in a specific historical period (historical recounts)
	Historical account	To account for why events occurred at a particular historical time
	Explanation sequential causal	To explain how and why processes occur in our social and physical worlds. Sequential explanations connect the events in a process chronologically. Causal explanations connect the events chronologically and causally
	Expository genres argument analytical hortatory discussion	To present arguments on an issue. An analytical argument attempts to persuade the reader/listener to agree with a particular point of view. An hortatory argument presents arguments and also tries to persuade the reader/listener to take some action. Discussions present the case for more than one point of view about an issue
	Procedure	To instruct someone to make or do things
Response genres	Personal response	To respond personally to a culturally significant work
	Review	To assess the appeal and value of a culturally significant work, providing some information about the text and evaluation
	Interpretation	To interpret what a culturally significant work is trying to say, providing some evidence from the work to support the interpretation
	Critical response	To critique a culturally significant work by analysing and making transparent the cultural values of the work, providing evidence....

Summary

The chapter has described the application of text-based curriculum design to a variety of contexts. The model is adaptable to different needs and circumstances, with flexibility for system-wide renewal of policies as well as for school-based programme development. The social theory of language not only underpins potential implementation of the design within diverse settings but also explains its adaptability to quite different conditions.

Notes and Readings

The models reviewed in this chapter suggest that texts as units of analysis are applicable to curriculum design in different contexts, even where there are institutional constraints. The models assume that teachers work with texts together with learners for authentic purposes. Teachers make decisions about programmes and create social environments for setting up connections with texts. Texts provide models and expressions for communication where teachers' oral proficiency is limited. They create a focus for working with large classes. But models vary in their applicability. Although bilingual programmes immerse students in language-rich environments and are powerful examples of social theory in action, community and institutional support is needed for their founding and maintenance. Establishing an extensive reading programme is both practical and efficient for language instruction – the interactive nature of reading immerses readers in how lexico-grammar works to make meaning – but the programme needs lots of books and texts and freedom for students to manage their own reading. The main point is that teaching with texts can be incorporated in a wide range of contexts.

Tasks

(1) The chapter outlines different curriculum applications. Review the examples and consider the advantages and disadvantages of the models which interest you.
(2) Which of the curriculum applications summarised in the chapter could be adapted to a teaching context with which you are familiar? What practical and administrative decisions would be needed to adapt and implement it in your situation?
(3) Document a curriculum model which implements a text-based design or aspects of one. This might be documenting your teaching programme as a first step to reporting it at a conference or as a research article.

(4) Imagine you would like to change the curriculum model in your institution or pilot a change with one class. Outline for colleagues the plan, the reasons for the change and the expected outcomes from making the change.
(5) Set up a small action research project to implement and evaluate an extended reading programme.

8 Curriculum Design in Higher Education: Planning Academic Programmes

Learning to write academic genres essentially means developing an understanding of the social practices of one's discipline, becoming aware of the functions of texts and how these functions are conventionally accomplished.... it requires that students gain an awareness of the discipline's symbolic resources for getting things done by routinely connecting purposes with features of texts.
Hyland (2004a: 145)

Introduction

Curriculum design was not a significant concern for higher education in the past. Academics selected content for a course or programme based on an agreed tradition of knowledge and skills which constituted an area of human experience and expertise. Today, curriculum design in higher education has become a priority for a number of reasons: the globalisation of education; market competition for students; international ranking of universities; the broadening intake of students from diverse backgrounds; and extending the access of minority groups to further education.

Management in tertiary education is aware of the need to reflect changes in society and to take account of the expectations of employers. Institutions of higher education are creating new cross-disciplinary subjects in response to changes in culture, technology and the environment, in lived and natural ecologies. Business communities demand training in specific workplace-linked literacy and numeracy practices, which are both highly complex and task specific, and require multi-skilling. International enrolments, implementation of online programmes and electronic assessment have put pressure on academics to design course delivery which is multimodal, which is accessed autonomously and which is not a replication of traditional lectures and tutorial activities.

For reasons of quality control, management in higher education is increasingly interventionist in pedagogy, in evaluation of teaching, in assessment procedures and in delivery of programmes. To control quality in electronic study environments, tertiary institutions have designed instruments for the measurement of effective teaching, have prescribed methods of instruction around descriptions of graduate skills and have mandated assessment procedures. The procedures associated with management of instruction have introduced metadiscourses which are parallel discourses to teachers' work and students' study and which are not obviously congruent or integral to disciplinary practices – to the epistemologies of subject-specific learning. They add complexity to the task of students' engagement with subject-specific practices and discourses. The changes impact directly on the curricula of specific disciplines, on what is taught and how it is taught, shaping disciplinary epistemologies and general notions of knowledge building, of enquiry-based learning and of skills development.

The purpose of this chapter is to set out a procedure for planning a curriculum in higher education which is integral to disciplinary and cross-disciplinary practices so that students encounter and engage with the knowledge and skills – with the discourses and modalities – which constitute academic practices. A focus on the curriculum in the context of change generates opportunities for academics to renew pedagogies and to create communities of critical and enthusiastic learners in ways that differ from those of the past. With the management of curriculum design, academics can create space to maintain the integrity of their fields of expertise and to explain the rationale for practices which constitute the epistemologies – the core knowledge and skills – of their disciplines.

Curriculum Design and Quality Teaching

Higher education is a global enterprise with institutions competing internationally for status and students. Pressure on lecturers to teach inclusively to the broadened cohort of students has shifted attention from transmission of knowledge and skills to providing access to and delivery of knowledge and skills through tasks and projects, utilising new technologies and modes of instruction. The proposal for curriculum design in this chapter is based on the concept of students' learning as academic apprenticeship into the social practices which define and differentiate the knowledge and skills of professional and technical communities. Students' academic engagement with skilled people and their practices is a process of socialisation into defined and distinctive communities. Students as newcomers to a course participate in activities with experts; they experience information in the context of the practices of the academic subject.

The internationalisation of education and widening access to higher education has created the need to focus on adult learning and how to communicate knowledge and skills. The quality of teaching has become a significant factor in the marketplace to attract students. Academics face practical questions of how to make instruction comprehensible to students new to the language, to local processes of education and to the epistemological culture of educational institutions.

Text-based curriculum design makes explicit for students the practices and the discourses integral to the development of subject-specific expertise. It sets a framework for education which aims to develop students' capabilities for participation in the academic community in which they are enrolled. A curriculum plan connects students with the practices of experts; it makes information accessible and responsive to students' needs; it creates environments for students' engagement with discourses and technical resources for work; and it utilises techniques of enquiry for students to investigate practices and to conduct research independently and in study groups. Through investigations, through problem-based learning and through the critical evaluation of information, students go beyond being consumers of research findings or observers of action. They become creators of knowledge, able to evaluate and critique information, and to access knowledge from different sources.

Academic Literacies

Academic study requires understanding and using specialised discourses for participation in disciplinary practices. Different academic domains require task-related literacies, engaging students in multiliteracies and multimodalities as members of disciplinary groups. Language competence is a significant factor in students' success in tertiary studies. Disciplinary knowledge or subject content is characterised with specific practices, discourses and text types (Bazerman, 1988; Swales, 1990). A curriculum focus on the language, on the discourses in tertiary education, on literacy and numeracy, recognises the role of language in learning and in the creation and communication of knowledge.

Academic knowledge and disciplinary epistemologies are characterised by discourse differentiation. Academic language comprises multiple texts and tasks embedded in disciplinary practices. The specific meanings of subjects are constituted by distinctive practices, such as drawing graphs, creating and composing designs, constructing models, writing texts and calculating profit and loss. Different texts have the essential function of integrating the multiple systems of meanings which comprise professions and disciplines. Discipline-specific discourses enable discipline-specific practices, such as writing a biography, classification of species, researching the functioning of T-rays, mapping environmental damage, and meta-programming software systems.

Students carry out coursework tasks and assignments with distinctive discourses (Halliday & Martin, 1993; Mickan, 2007; Teramoto & Mickan, 2008). A social theory of learning describes people's socialisation or apprenticeship into the practices and semiotic resources of communities. Applied to academic studies, social theory describes students' study and learning of knowledge or skills as a process of socialisation – a process of engagement in the social practices of a discipline or specialist subject by taking part in the conventional and defining activities of that discipline, with the texts – the discourses – and materials and tools (the semiotic resources) of that discipline.

Students' expertise is exhibited in the proficiency with which they understand and express knowledge and apply skills within the context of their studies. Students new to a discipline or a subject in a discipline face new texts, which they need to comprehend to compose contributions in seminars and presentations and to formulate responses in assignments. Explicitness about the text types and the wordings which constitute texts and tasks is essential. Through interactions with community members, people learn meanings and uses of resources for the enactment of social practices (Mickan, 2006). From the perspective of curriculum planning, new students are in the position of apprentices who need to develop discourse resources in order to take part in the practices of the academic communities in which they are enrolled.

Disciplinary Knowledge

Academics in tertiary education are discipline experts, who plan programmes of work and determine assessment based upon experience and agreed practices. They select the subject content, which a discipline community develops over time as a core body of specialist knowledge and range of skills. Disciplinary knowledge comprises the topics or the information needed to display scholarship in a disciplinary domain. Disciplines with traditions of instruction and pathways of study and records of research have established academic credentials, which provide models of practice for lecturers to follow and for students to develop. Theory and practice are interconnected as students develop skills for research, for design, for construction and for technical applications. Disciplines with a professional focus incorporate workplace activities. There is a clarity about what students need to do.

Alongside and interwoven with the core tertiary subjects offered by a university are new areas of human experience and academic work, integrating knowledge and practices from different disciplines with new discourses.

Epistemologies of subjects and disciplinary boundaries are redefined with incorporation of content from different disciplines. Technologies are part of the change, contributing to the construction of new areas of knowledge and shaping how content is delivered. The epistemological changes are constituted by different practices and carried out with different discourses – the very essence of new curriculum subjects. The question is, what does this mean for students and what are the implications for instruction?

When students' work across disciplinary boundaries, they engage with discourses and other semiotic resources with different requirements and expectations. A traditional essay is replaced with a research project. Assignments comprise multimedia reports and PowerPoint presentations. In order to take part in the academic practices of a particular course, students need to manage and control discourses across disciplines. Cross-disciplinary changes have implications for students' experiences for learning and for instructors for curriculum design: What content is selected for inclusion in a new course and what is the process for selection? How are assessment tasks moulded? Do they draw upon different source disciplines? The subject used as an example in this chapter comes from a postgraduate award in Geographical and Environmental Studies. The purpose of this chapter is to illustrate a procedure for determining curriculum practices and texts as the basis for academic curriculum design.

Disciplinary knowledge and curriculum design

The procedure for curriculum design is based on the epistemology of a subject. This is established by asking questions about the nature of work in the subject: What is it to be an historian? Or what is it to be an electronic engineer? What semiotic resources does an apprentice student need for the development of expert practices as an electronic engineer? The task is to identify the significant practices of an expert practitioner in the disciplinary area.

The steps in the procedure are illustrated in Figure 8.1. The first stage is defining content of the subject. What is to be taught as a priority? What is it to be an expert in the subject area? The epistemology is described by mapping valued knowledge and skills in the subject. Syllabus statements of subjects are typical representations of the valued content. Table 8.1 states the aims and outcomes for the subject 'environmental impact assessment' (EIA), which is a postgraduate programme in Geographical and Environmental Studies. What students need to do to accomplish the course requirements is summarised in the aims, outcomes and graduate attributes. These general statements of the subject are abstractions of the actual practices students

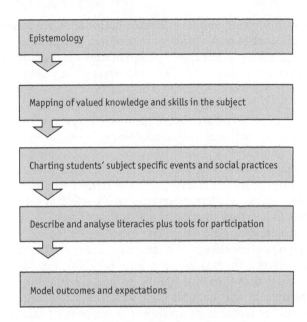

Figure 8.1 Academic curriculum design procedure

Table 8.1 Aims and outcomes for the subject 'environmental impact assessment' (EIA)

Topic aims	Learning outcomes/graduate attributes
1. Develop an understanding of the purpose, process and methods of EIA	1. Explain the history, context, methods and various stages of the EIA process
2. Show the critical role of EIA processes in different states of Australia and in other countries	2. Comprehend the role of EIA in environmental management and for achieving the goal of sustainable development
3. Highlight the variability of EIA processes in different states of Australia and in other countries	3. Critically assess the usefulness, strengths and limitations of the EIA process
4. Draw attention to the strengths and weaknesses of the EIA process	4. Discuss the social, ecological, political and economic dimensions of the EIA process
5. Further develop critical thinking skills or ecological literacy with regard to developmental and environmental issues	5. Communicate effectively about concepts, ideas and issues of the EIA process

Table 8.2 Learning outcomes/graduate attributes, linked to literacy practices and texts, for the subject 'environmental impact assessment' (EIA)

Learning outcomes/graduate attributes	Minimum of literacy practices and texts
1. Explain the history, context, methods and various stages of the EIA process	Review of literature; reading textbooks and articles; selecting relevant information; writing explanatory text and procedural text
2. Comprehend the role of EIA in environmental management and for achieving the goal of sustainable development	Reading topic-specific literature; listening and interpreting information in lectures and seminars
3. Critically assess the usefulness, strengths and limitations of the EIA process	Reading relevant texts; selection and noting of information; composing a structured argument essay
4. Discuss the social, ecological, political and economic dimensions of the EIA process	Relevant reading of books and articles; selection of applicable information; oral argumentation in seminars; composition of discussion texts
5. Communicate effectively about concepts, ideas and issues of the EIA process	Oral discussions and explanations; written assignments; seminar presentations

need to accomplish to demonstrate management of the epistemology – the knowledge and skills – of the subject.

The statements of outcomes and attributes expose the centrality of language for the display of competence in the subject. Specifically, they show a set of texts students need for the display of competence; for example, the most apparent are explanations, procedures, reports, critiques, discussions, negotiations and presentations. Each of these represents distinctive text types, with relevant formats and wording selections. To illustrate this, Table 8.2 matches probable texts with the learning outcomes/graduate attributes for the same EIA subject.

It is in the specific encounters and social practices of the subject that the significance of the experiences of texts is revealed. This is framed in the same subject, EIA, with a series of questions: What are the main events students need to take part in for apprenticeship into the field of environmental impact assessment? What study and teaching events are necessary for the apprenticeship of students? What 'literacy events' constitute the course? The representation of literacy events in Figure 8.2 summarises the main subject-specific practices that students are expected to join in for the acquisition of subject knowledge and skills. In a cross-disciplinary subject like

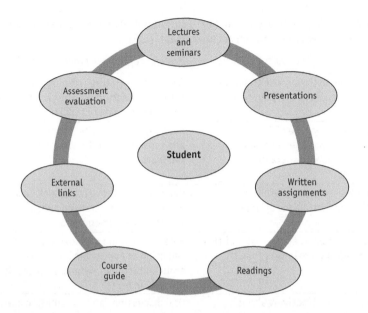

Figure 8.2 Representation of literacy events in EIA (Mickan *et al.*, 2009)

EIA, the traditional texts of geography, such as maps, classifications and descriptions of landforms, have been expanded with the introduction of textual practices for project evaluation. The specific content of the subject is constituted with multiple literacy events and practices, with spoken and written discourses incorporating visual modalities in presentations and lectures.

Students' success in their academic studies requires the application of knowledge and skills in the accomplishment of specific practices. For EIA, the professional consultant is required to obtain data, evaluate the data and related information, and report with recommendations. This is carried out with technical discourses. For the purposes of the apprenticeship, students conduct EIAs tailored to course timelines and conditions. The questions framing the curriculum also determine the assessment tasks: What literacy practices demonstrate expert participation in the professional community? In what texts does a student need to display competence in the performance of the social practices? In this way assessment tasks are specified in terms of practices related to subject knowledge and skills.

The naming of disciplinary practices and the discourses which constitute the academic community reveals the core events of students' apprenticeship in the shared knowledge and skills of the disciplinary community. The listing represents the practical nature of knowledge and skill acquisition and makes the curriculum explicit for students. It also clarifies the general descriptions of aims, outcomes and graduate attributes, as the naming raises awareness of the range of text types required for the participation of students in the subject-specific practices. Students are positioned to distinguish the literacy tasks embedded in specific events – in the lectures, seminars and presentations – and the texts associated with academic study.

Summary

In cross-disciplinary courses, students' work requires management of multiple literacies across modalities. Making explicit the distinctive patterns in the wording of texts enables students to see the defining features of language needed to carry out tasks (Figure 8.3). Introduction to the wording of specific texts connected to the purposes for which they are written supports students' analysis of tasks and provides a basis for assessment and for measuring outcomes. This awareness of text is important for students

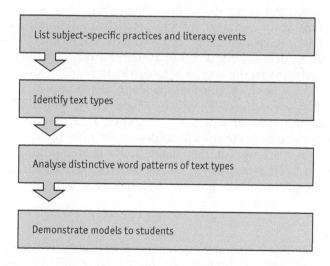

List subject-specific practices and literacy events

Identify text types

Analyse distinctive word patterns of text types

Demonstrate models to students

Figure 8.3 Procedure for analysis of discipline specific academic literacies

with language experiences different from the particular academic course. As students display the fulfilment of tasks through various literacy events, criteria for assessment can include the extent to which text features meet specifications.

Subject-specific information for students is based on mapping of literacy events and practices, identification of text types, analysis of the distinctive word patterns of texts, and model texts or exemplars for students to review.

An understanding of subject-specific practices and associated discourses is a way into teaching academic content and skills. The academic integrity of the curriculum and instructional practices are foregrounded with the analysis of subject knowledge and skills as practices, mediated in literacies and in other modalities.

Notes and Readings

The focus of this chapter is on the discourses of academic subjects. This is a well researched area. Bazerman's (1988) study of the genre and activity of articles reporting experimental science has been influential for later work on academic texts. Swales' (1990) research on academic communities and genres has generated research into academic literacy. Paltridge (2001) related genre theory to language teaching. Hyland (2004a) used concordancing programs to identify text features of disciplines, basing the analysis on subject-specific corpora. The use of concordancing programs to analyse the features of text types and of disciplinary discourses is a practical way into the identification of wordings characteristic of a subject and discipline (Adams, 2006). Ravelli and Ellis (2005) edited a collection of essays on the analysis of academic writing using systemic functional linguistics. The essays are relevant to the approach to curriculum design and text analysis outlined in this book. The same applies to the essays in the collection edited by McCabe et al. (2009), which includes essays on multiliteracies and multimodalities, both of which are recognised as significant for academic work. Essays also examine voice in academic discourse and the use of corpus linguistics for teaching. Another theoretically related series of studies are published in O'Halloran (2004), on multimodal discourse analysis, which applies systemic functional linguistics perspectives to the analysis.

Tasks

(1) Hyland (2005: 196) states: 'Scholarly discourse … is not uniform and monolithic but an outcome of a multitude of different practices and strategies'. Choose two different academic subjects; identify the core

literacy practices and discourses, record them, describe some of the main patterns of discourse and compare them. Report the analysis in a seminar.

(2) Introduce students to the use of a discipline-specific corpus for analysis and for composition of texts. Select representative texts of a discipline or an academic subject to build a corpus of texts, then introduce students to the use of a concordancing program to explore wordings which characterise the texts.

(3) Select a higher-education course or subject and document or map the social practices which students are required to take part in. What are the practices which are central to the subject? What literacy practices constitute the subject and what texts are students required to manage for displaying entry to the particular academic community?

(4) Choose two different subjects, if possible from different disciplines, and compare text types which are supposedly the same, such as an essay in psychology and in philosophy. What are the similarities in the structure of the text types and what are the differences? What features exemplify the epistemology of each subject?

(5) The article by Teramoto and Mickan (2008), 'Writing a critical review: Reflections on literacy practices', documents the literacy practices of writing an assignment. Use the article as a model for the documentation and analysis of one assignment or task in an academic course; write a report on the analysis for a seminar discussion.

9 Language Planning, Curriculum Renewal and the Teacher as Researcher

> *What is common to every use of language is that it is meaningful,*
> *contextualised, and in the broadest sense social....*
> Halliday, in Webster (2009: 207)

Introduction

Language planning in education involves the development and implementation of official policies on children's linguistic education. The previous chapters introduced a social semiotic theory of language and learning as the basis for the design of curricula in general – with language education as the specific instance. The proposal for curriculum renewal assumes a reappraisal of policy and practice in language education. Instead of patching up a linguistic framework with elements of discourse in order to achieve a communicative curriculum, the suggestion is that change at a theoretical level is needed to inform and invigorate language programmes. The suggested process involves a review of both the theory of what is language and what it is to learn a language. Change of this kind implicates educational institutions in language planning – in the review of language policies and practices. The chapter considers curriculum renewal in relation to language planning from three perspectives: language policy and curriculum design; programme structure; and teacher education and professional development.

Language planning is designed to link theory, policy and practice. A curriculum model based on a social theory of learning with texts as units of analysis is designed to create a coherent procedure for planning policy, programmes and practices. It addresses some of the contradictions in programmes designed to develop communicative skills, such as the assessment of grammar apart from texts. Based on a semiotic concept of language and learning, language planning can be used to revitalise learners' language experiences. The theory has applications to curriculum planning in different contexts, for programmes with different purposes. It applies to language education programmes in general: to first- and second- and additional-languages programmes, to literacy and numeracy programmes, to language

maintenance and revival programmes, and to research in language development and education.

Planning Curriculum Renewal

The purpose of language planning is to establish coherent programmes
across theory, policy and practice. For some communicative language
teaching (CLT) programmes this was not the case. CLT programmes described
communicative goals and outcomes, which, however, were assessed for
grammatical accuracy, for example in national tests. Teachers were con-
fronted with this contradiction in the delivery of programmes. Curriculum
statements advocated the development of communicative skills through
authentic interaction, but assessment systems tested accuracy of discrete
items of grammar in decontextualised sentences or with multiple-choice
tests. Teachers faced the dilemma of preparing students for grammatical
tests at the expense of communicative activities. The contradictions and
unrealistic expectations both frustrated teachers and disillusioned learners.
The application of social semiotic theory to curriculum design supports
the integration of grammatical analysis with cultural knowledge and with
discourse resources for communication.

Policy, goals and outcomes

A language planning perspective requires the review of existing policies
and practices, specifies a rationale for change in policy and programmes, and
sets out a plan for implementation. Each stage or component of planning
is informed by a language theory and learning theory. In a text-based curriculum the foundation for policy planning is the concept of language as
a meaning-making resource. The general purpose of learning languages is
to develop the verbal capacity for the comprehension and expression of
meanings. Programme goals describe learning in terms of participation
in the social practices of communities with texts and other resources –
material, visual and spatial. Context and language use are interconnected
with learners' participation in the literacy and oracy practices of general or
specified communities of practice – a class, a workplace team, a friendship
group or a committee. Participation takes place with texts and possibly
other semiotic resources. The description of goals and objectives in terms of
participation in practices with texts sets realistic objectives for learners and
specificity for the selection of programme content.

For general-language programmes in schools, the identification of
goals appears not as obvious as for specific-purpose target communities:
there is disagreement over notions of authenticity and purposefulness of

learners' classroom experiences, with commentators suggesting that the authenticity derives from aspirations or plans related to future travel and further study – in other words, for use of the language outside of school. But school lessons are sites for routine language use for practical purposes, in which language is normally the significant means of communication. In lessons participants use language which is socially situated – a class is a community in which business is conducted with multiple literacy and oracy discourses. Lessons provide scope for making curriculum choices appropriate to teachers' and learners' interests and needs. Although for introductory language programmes, statements of goals, practices and texts need to vary in response to class community skills and interests, for programmes such as English for academic purposes (EAP), English for specific purposes (ESP) and content-based programmes the practices and texts of a target community can be described with relative clarity. The goals are explained in terms of participation in language practices for community membership. The units of analysis for the description of objectives are texts or distinctive discourses pertaining to community social practices – the literacy and oracy practices which mark out participation. In this system designers and programmers harmonise and synchronise the development of written and oral skills by integrating them in text-based tasks. The grammar or wording of texts – the lexico-grammar – is contextualised and actualised in texts, providing real contexts for analysis of grammar and for the expression of particular meanings for different purposes. Assessment tasks are based on texts, so that testing practices are consistent with programme goals, teaching activities and outcomes. Stages of language development involve descriptions of text-based activities, which extend the range of learners' literacy and oral practices for participation in the particular community.

Language Planning for Curriculum Renewal

This section addresses several questions relevant to planning policies and programmes in education. Policies on goals, syllabuses, entry to programmes and length of programmes are formulated in school education language plans. These include policies on levels of schooling at which teaching of languages commences, on programme content and goals, and on teacher training and professional development.

Programmes in early education

There is a general belief that the learning of additional languages in early-childhood programmes has advantages over language study by older learners. Young children respond enthusiastically and unselfconsciously to new language, and they pronounce language with accuracy. In a very natural way they pick up discourses in their social environment. This suggests that commencement of language courses earlier in school programmes or even in pre-school programmes is better than later. However, certain conditions need to be considered for the success of early-childhood languages programmes. These include teachers' expertise and language proficiency, programme content and authenticity of discourse, and learners' pathways for progression across year levels in planned programmes.

Teachers' expertise and language proficiency have a crucial role in language programmes which are designed to develop language use in early education. Teachers' confidence in the use of a target language enables the implementation of teaching approaches congruent with children's earliest experiences of language as discourse – that is, language used purposefully in contexts for the comprehension and expression of meanings. The idea is that the teacher's instruction promotes making meaning through language. For teachers confident in speaking the target language, lessons will be normal sites for working together orally and for reciting and reading and discussing functional texts together. For teachers with more confidence in the written language than in oral interactions, relevant and engaging written texts comprise the focus for work in lessons, using where available recorded texts on iPhones, on tablets or as pod casts. Written and recorded texts provide a resource for comment and discussion, including for texting and chatting on Twitter.

The selection of programme content influences the authenticity of discourse in early-childhood programmes. Some policies for languages in the first years of schooling recommend initially teaching language orally, rather than introducing reading and writing. It is assumed that beginners need to learn some phrases and word lists even though these may lack coherent meanings. It is also assumed that language teachers of young children require limited proficiency to teach vocabulary and simple expressions. But a major role of education in elementary schools is literacy instruction associated with broadening learners' discourse repertoire. The combination of oral and literacy activities provides children with rich and varied experiences of texts. Teachers actively read and talk about and around texts with children. Early literacy experiences form the foundation for children's work with texts, which serve as resources for children's participation in a class community, in which they share meanings and compose texts together.

Children's interest and motivation are influenced by the experience of making advances in comprehension of texts and expression of meanings. Structuring pathways for learners' progression across year levels are the basis for the success of programmes. A planned curriculum facilitates progression in language development across levels of schooling. As with other areas of the curriculum, learners need to engage with an expanding range of texts constituting new domains of experience – new topics, new tasks, new techniques and new technological applications. Children perceive the long pathway of learning an additional language as worthwhile and rewarding when they experience consistent growth in their communicative ability. The value of programmes for young learners which extend over year levels is the opportunity to achieve advanced proficiency in the language.

Curriculum renewal, teacher education and professional development

Teacher education and professional development are integral components of language planning for curriculum change. In practical terms, changing a curriculum from grammatical analysis, and from word- and sentence-level exercises, to working with texts is difficult. If instruction is dependent on textbooks which claim to be communicative but retain grammar as a focus in exercises, the shift to a teacher-managed curriculum is challenging. Where local or national examinations include testing of grammar isolated from texts, regardless of meaning, preparation for assessment remains a priority. Even in circumstances in which teachers have options to design their own courses, the shift from grammar-based to text-based pedagogy requires a fundamental rethink of how to organise programmes and lessons.

For pre-service education, a coherent theory of language and learning is the foundation for the implementation of a social semiotic approach to curriculum design. The practical focus for trainee teachers is the analysis of everyday language as well as technical texts related to academic study and workplace communication. The central concept is the relationship of texts to contexts – the study of texts and the social practices with which they are associated. The identification of text types focuses on the configuration of wordings which typify particular social practices. Grammatical analysis focuses on the word choices in texts which realise typical social purposes. Educational programmes build trainees' awareness of language in daily use, as they document and examine the kinds of texts which constitute participation in communities, and the specific language choices which fulfil different purposes and functions in communities. The transcriptions of spoken texts and the collection of written and visual texts are resources for analysis, for discussion and as the resource for composition of learners' own texts, and for the design of curriculum and assessment protocols.

For practising teachers, in-service training or professional development for curriculum renewal is more complex. Implementation of policy impacts directly on institutional requirements and on teaching practices. The roles of teachers in the management of language programmes vary from facilitators implementing externally designed curriculum to directors and class teachers with responsibility for the development and delivery of a local curriculum. The roles determine the extent to which an individual teacher adapts or develops programmes appropriate to local learners' circumstances and aspirations.

Teachers who manage their own curriculum and who determine course content have the option to negotiate and craft a flexible, text-based programme. It enables the design of tasks relevant and challenging for learners with access to multiple texts for the analysis of text types related to social function. Teachers with minimal management control over programme content or assessment may review a course or set textbook and consider the inclusion of additional or optional texts to augment learners' discourse repertoire. It may be possible to restructure a programme around authentic texts which incorporate specified grammatical or lexical items in national tests or textbooks. This approach would enrich learners' participation in text-based activities and at the same time match programme objectives.

For the implementation of language policies and plans, teachers need time and support in order to review practices and to design, to select and to prepare texts for lesson activities. Having the teacher act as a researcher, applying qualitative investigative methods, is a practical and focused procedure for professional development. At a classroom level, teachers are change agents, whose professional development involves analysis of their own practices. Lessons are primary sites for the documentation, analysis and evaluation of oral and literacy practices. Through action research, teachers apply a manageable process of planning, enacting and reviewing change in their classroom practices. Such school-based enquiry is relevant to teachers' work. Through their investigations teachers collaboratively create and accumulate understanding, expertise and skills for teaching with texts as a professional activity.

Notes and Readings

Mühlhäusler (2000) has framed language planning within an ecological paradigm. He locates the discussion of language planning within environmental and cultural settings. He writes:

> The ecological approach [to language planning] sees human communication embedded in a complex socio-historical, spatial and interpersonal

> ecology. Its basic assumption is that meaning is created not because inter-locutors share a code but because there are relations between them that enable them to arrive at an agreed meaning. (Mühlhäusler, 2000: 331)

The ecolinguistic perspective focuses planners' attention on the contexts of language programmes, taking into consideration the interrelationship of language, environment and human activity. Such an integrated paradigm has implications for the planning of language programmes in education, both for the teaching of additional languages and for the revival and main-tenance of local and indigenous languages.

There is a lot of work to be done to develop, trial and evaluate text-based curricula in the implementation of a social semiotic curriculum. Joyce and Burns (1999) provide a practical examination of different approaches to teaching grammar, with suggestions for the study of texts in context.

Halliday's systemic functional linguistics (SFL) is the theory which underpins text-based curriculum design (Mickan, 2011). *The Collected Works of M.A.K. Halliday* edited by J. Webster (2003–2009) have been published by Continuum, London. There are many publications written for teaching SFL. Introductory texts include Butt *et al.* (2000) and Derewianka (2011).

For further information on the numerous publications and research studies based on SFL, check out the website of the Australian Systemic Functional Linguistics Association (ASFLA), http://www.asfla.org.au/.

Tasks

(1) *Evaluation of programmes.* A starting point for curriculum change in policy and practices is the analysis of current programmes. The analysis is based on an evaluation of programme aims, objectives and assessment for consistency and coherence. The analysis can be applied to national policy statements, to regional language plans, to school programmes and to the content of textbooks in relation to assessment practices.

(2) *Documentation of lessons.* Teachers are in the best position to review their own practices through documenting programme content and recording of lessons. The kinds of questions which teachers might explore include: What texts do students read, write and talk about in language programmes? How normal or authentic is the language which students use? What structures and word choices distinguish texts used for different purposes?

(3) *Investigations into text-based instruction.* Lessons are events for investiga-tion of work with texts as they are occasions for the study of language choice, for variety of texts and for the authenticity of interactions.

Observing and recording students working together with texts offers the potential for noting how work on the meanings of texts triggers the exchange of ideas and an exploration of meanings in authentic interaction.

(4) *Expanding experiences of texts.* With access to content through iPhones, iPads, podcasts and other electronic media, students connect with current texts and topics for debate, for analysis and for fun. Students select texts according to type, purpose and topic for use in class. Document the range and use of different texts chosen by students.

(5) *Professional experience and action research.* Teachers' own research has developed our understanding of the intricacies of instruction in lessons. Action research is a professional process of self-analysis during which a practitioner identifies an issue, an innovation or an option for action arising from practical experiences. As action researchers, teachers both document their practices and ·identify specific, relevant aspects of instruction for change. The approach is a realistic and appropriate means for teachers to make changes in working with students for the implementation of a text-based curriculum.

Conclusion

The review of curriculum change over the last few decades (Chapter 2) highlights two factors. The first factor is teachers' and researchers' increasing understanding of what it is to communicate and therefore what it is to teach additional languages. Language as texts is functional in the contexts of social practices. It is no longer sufficient for programmes with communicative goals to teach and test items of grammar in isolation from texts. The second factor is the expansion of language items included in programmes when a curriculum adds discourse elements to traditional grammar to make it more communicative, with functions, speech acts, phrases or tasks. This has increased the complexity of teachers' planning and work. Hence the need for language planning which in a systematic way examines assumptions about language and learning. Since humans work with texts, a practical approach to curriculum renewal for the enhancement of teachers' and students' language experiences is the formulation of the curriculum around textual practices. The implementation of a text-based curriculum is efficient, realistic and sensible.

The review or evaluation of existing policies and practices underlies the language curriculum planning procedure proposed in this book A starting point is the analysis of existing language policies and plans, in order to achieve consistency and coherence between aims and objectives and assessment. A problem in language education has been the contradiction between policies which aim to develop the language proficiency skills of students, but assess students' competency with minimalist scales such as multiple-choice tests, grammatical accuracy in sentences and knowledge of words in isolation from texts. What is apparent from this experience is the discrepancy between goals and procedures. Also problematic has been the 'patch-up the curriculum' approach applied to make programmes more communicative by simply adding functions, notions, speech acts and genres without a fundamental reappraisal of the nature of language use and of language learning and therefore of instructional practices.

Language planning at national and local levels is the institutional means for curriculum renewal. The aim is the creation of language programmes in which children and students observe and study the texts of a language in action in the social practices of class communities, in workplaces and in everyday social and leisure activities. Through observation and analysis, learners participate in textual practices for the comprehension and expression of relevant meanings. The aim is for learners to engage with texts – with the analysis of texts and their social function in relevant spheres of human activity – which excite, enhance and extend their meaning-making potential.

References

Adams, R. (2006) Developing professional phraseology: A corpus linguistics approach. In P. Mickan, I. Petrescu and J. Timoney (eds) *Social Practices, Pedagogy and Language Use: Studies in Socialisation* (pp. 72–82). Adelaide: Lythrum Press.

Adelaide Secondary School of English (2006) *Pathway: A Science Curriculum.* Adelaide: Adelaide Secondary School of English.

Baker, C. (1993) *Foundations of Bilingual Education and Bilingualism.* Clevedon: Multilingual Matters.

Bazerman, C. (1988) *Shaping Written Knowledge: The Genre and Activity of the Experimental Article in Science.* Madison, WI: University of Wisconsin Press.

Butt, D., Fahey, R., Feez, S., Spinks, S. and Yallop, C. (2000) *Using Functional Grammar: An Explorer's Guide* (2nd edn). Sydney: National Centre for English Language Teaching and Research, Macquarie University.

Callaghan, M., Knapp, P. and Noble, G. (1993) Genre in practice. In B. Cope and M. Kalantzis (eds) *The Powers of Literacy. A Genre Approach to Teaching Writing* (pp. 179–202). London: Falmer Press.

Christie, F. and Martin, J. (2000) *Genre and Institutions: Social Processes in the Workplace and School.* London: Continuum.

Cloran, C., Butt, D. and Williams, G. (eds) (1996) *Ways of Saying: Ways of Meaning. Selected Papers of Ruqaiya Hasan.* London: Cassell.

Cope, B. and Kalantzis, M. (eds) (1993) *The Powers of Literacy: A Genre Approach to Teaching Writing.* London: Falmer Press.

Crookes, G. and Gass, S. (eds) (1993a) *Tasks in a Pedagogical Context: Integrating Theory and Practice.* Clevedon: Multilingual Matters.

Crookes, G. and Gass, S. (eds) (1993b) *Tasks and Language Learning: Integrating Theory and Practice.* Clevedon: Multilingual Matters.

Department of Education, Training and Employment (DETE) (2005) *ESL Scope and Scales.* Adelaide: DETE.

Derewianka, B. (2011) *A New Grammar Companion for Teachers.* Sydney: Primary English Teaching Association Australia.

De Zarobe, Y. and Catalan, R. (2009) *Content and Language Integrated Learning.* Bristol: Multilingual Matters.

Duranti, A. and Goodwin, C. (1995) *Rethinking Context: Language as an Interactive Phenomenon.* Cambridge: Cambridge University Press.

Eggins, S. (1994) *An Introduction to Systemic Functional Linguistics.* London: Pinter.

Eggins, S. and Slade, D. (1997) *Analysing Casual Conversation.* London: Cassell.

Feez, S. (1998) *Text-Based Syllabus Design.* Sydney: National Centre for English Language Teaching and Research, Macquarie University.

130

Finocchiaro, M. and Brumfit, C. (1983) *The Functional–Notional Approach: From Theory to Practice*. Oxford: Oxford University Press.

Gale, M. and Mickan, P. (2008) Nripun your ko:pi: We want more than body parts, but how? In R. Amery and J. Nash (eds) *Warra Wiltaniappendi: Strengthening Languages* (pp. 81–88). Adelaide: Print Junction.

Gee, J. (1990) *Social Linguistics and Literacies: Ideology in Discourses*. London: Falmer Press.

Gibbons, P. (2006) *Bridging Discourses in the ESL Classroom: Students, Teachers and Researchers*. London: Continuum.

Halliday, M. (1973) *Explorations in the Functions of Language*. London: Edward Arnold.

Halliday, M. (1975) *Learning How to Mean: Explorations in the Development of Language*. London: Edward Arnold.

Halliday M. (1978) *Language as Social Semiotic: The Social Interpretation of Language and Meaning*. London: Edward Arnold.

Halliday, M. (1985) *Spoken and Written Language*. Geelong: Deakin University Press.

Halliday, M. (1994) *An Introduction to Functional Grammar* (4th edn). London: Edward Arnold.

Halliday, M. (2004) *An Introduction to Functional Grammar*. London: Hodder Education.

Halliday, M. and Hasan, R. (1985) *Language, Context and Text: Aspects of Language in a Social–Semiotic Perspective*. Geelong: Deakin University Press.

Halliday, M. and Martin, J. (eds) (1993) *Writing Science: Literacy and Discursive Power*. London: Falmer Press.

Harris, R. (1996) *Signs, Language and Communication: Integrational and Segregational Approaches*. London: Routledge.

Hasan, R. and Williams, G. (1996) *Literacy in Society*. London: Longman.

Hodge, R. and Kress, G. (1988) *Social Semiotics*. Cambridge: Polity Press.

Hyland, K. (2004a) *Disciplinary Discourses: Social Interactions in Academic Writing* (2nd edn). Ann Arbor, MI: University of Michigan Press.

Hyland, K. (2004b) *Genre and Second Language Writing*. Ann Arbor, MI: University of Michigan Press.

Johnson, K. (1982) *Communicative Syllabus Design and Methodology*. Oxford: Pergamon Press.

Joyce, H. and Burns, A. (1999) *Focus on Grammar*. Sydney: National Centre for English Language Teaching and Research, Macquarie University.

Kennedy, B. (1959) *The Revised Latin Primer*. London: Longman.

Kim, D. (2006) Extensive reading for EFL students in Korea. In P. Mickan, I. Petrescu and J. Timoney (eds) *Social Practices, Pedagogy and Language Use: Studies in Socialisation* (pp. 24–40). Adelaide: Lythrum Press.

Kramsch, C. (ed.) (2002) *Language Acquisition and Language Socialization*. London: Continuum.

Lantolf, J. (ed.) (2000) *Sociocultural Theory and Second Language Learning*. Oxford: Oxford University Press.

Lim, M. (2006) Discourse of the language classroom in Korea. In P. Mickan, I. Petrescu and J. Timoney (eds) *Social Practices, Pedagogy and Language Use: Studies in Socialisation* (pp. 41–56). Adelaide: Lythrum Press.

Lim, M. (2007) Exploring social practices in English classes: A qualitative investigation of classroom talk in a Korean secondary school. PhD thesis, University of Adelaide.

Littlewood, W. (1981) *Communicative Language Teaching: An Introduction*. Cambridge: Cambridge University Press.

Malinowski, B. (1994) The problem of meaning in primitive language. In J. Maybin (ed.) *Language and Literacy in Social Practice* (pp. 1–10). Clevedon: Multilingual Matters.

Martin, J. and Rose, D. (2005) *Working with Discourse: Meaning Beyond the Clause* (reprint). London: Continuum.

Martin, J. and Rose, D. (2008) *Genre Relations: Mapping Culture*. London: Equinox Publishing.

Maybin, J. (1994) Children's voices: Talk, knowledge and identity. In D. Graddol, J. Maybin and B. Stierer (eds) *Researching Language and Literacy in Social Context* (pp. 131–150). Clevedon: Multilingual Matters.

McCabe, A., O'Donnell, M. and Whittaker, R. (eds) (2009) *Advances in Language and Education*. London: Continuum.

McCarthy, M. (1991) *Discourse Analysis for Language Teachers*. Cambridge: Cambridge University Press.

McCarthy, M. and Carter, R. (1994) *Language as Discourse: Perspectives for Language Teaching*. Longman: London.

Mickan, P. (2000) Textualising meanings: Second language writers in action. PhD thesis, University of Adelaide.

Mickan, P. (2003) Beyond grammar: Text as unit of analysis. In J. James (ed.) *Grammar in the Language Classroom: Changing Approaches and Practices* (pp. 220–227). Singapore: SEAMEO Regional Language Centre.

Mickan, P. (2004) Teaching methodologies. In C. Conlan (ed.) *Teaching English in Australia: Theoretical Perspectives and Practical Issues* (pp. 171–191). Perth: API Network, Australia Research Institute.

Mickan, P. (2006) Socialisation, social practices and teaching. In P. Mickan, I. Petrescu and J. Timoney (eds) *Social Practices, Pedagogy and Language Use: Studies in Socialisation* (pp. 7–23). Adelaide: Lythrum Press.

Mickan, P. (2007) Doing science and home economics: Curriculum socialisation of new arrivals to Australia. *Language and Education*, 21 (1), 1–17.

Mickan, P. (2011) Text-based pedagogy and functional grammar. In S. Fukuda and H. Sakata (eds) *Monograph on Foreign Language Education*. Tokushima: Tokushima University.

Mickan, P., Medvedeva, K. and Wanner, T. (2009) Literacy practices in interdisciplinary studies. Paper presented at Linguistics Research Forum, University of Adelaide, 5–6 November.

Mickan, P., Petrescu, I. and Timoney, J. (eds) (2006) *Social Practices, Pedagogy and Language Use: Studies in Socialisation*. Adelaide: Lythrum Press.

Mühlhäusler, P. (2000) Language planning and language ecology. *Current Issues in Language Planning*, 1 (3), 306–367.

Mühlhäusler, P. (2003) *Language and Environment, Environment of Language: A Course in Ecolinguistics*. London: Battlebridge.

Munby, J. (1978) *Communicative Syllabus Design*. Cambridge: Cambridge University Press.

Nation, I. and Macalister, J. (2010) *Language Curriculum Design*. London: Routledge.

Nunan, D. (1988a) *Syllabus Design*. Oxford: Oxford University Press.

Nunan, D. (1988b) *The Learner-Centred Curriculum*. Cambridge: Cambridge University Press.

Nunan, D. (1989) *Designing Tasks for the Communicative Classroom*. Cambridge: Cambridge University Press.

O'Halloran, K. (ed.) (2004) *Multimodal Discourse Analysis: Systemic Functional Perspectives*. London: Continuum.

Okawa, T. (2008) Academic literacies in the discipline of nursing: Grammar as a resource for producing texts. Unpublished MA applied linguistics dissertation, University of Adelaide.

Orton, E. (1968) *Auf Deutsch, bitte!* London: George Harrap.

Paltridge, B. (2001) *Genre and the Language Learning Classroom.* Ann Arbor, MI: University of Michigan Press.

Paltridge, B. (2006) *Discourse Analysis.* London: Continuum.

Ravelli, L. and Ellis, R. (eds) (2005) *Analysing Academic Writing: Contextualized Frameworks.* London: Continuum.

Rothery, J. (1996) Making the changes: Developing an educational linguistics. In R. Hasan and G. Williams (eds) *Literacy in Society* (pp. 86–123). London: Longman.

St Brigid's School (2003) *Curriculum.* Kilburn: Catholic Education.

Schieffelin, B. and Ochs, E. (1986) Language socialisation. *Annual Review of Anthropology,* 15, 163–191.

Senior Secondary Assessment Board of South Australia (SSABSA) (2006) *Stage 1 and 2 English: Curriculum Statements.* Wayville: SSABSA.

Stillar, G. (1998) *Analyzing Everyday Texts: Discourse, Rhetoric, and Social Perspectives.* London: Sage Publications.

Swales, J. (1990) *Genre Analysis: English in Academic and Research Settings.* Cambridge: Cambridge University Press.

Tasmania Department of Education (2010a) The Tasmanian Statement on English. Online document at http://www.education.tas.gov.au/curriculum/standards/english/english/teachers/rationale.

Tasmania Department of Education (2010b) Texts. Online document at http://www.education.tas.gov.au/curriculum/standards/english/english/teachers/texts.

Teramoto, H. and Mickan, P. (2008) Writing a critical review: Reflections on literacy practices. *Language Awareness,* 17:1, 44–56.

Unsworth, L. (ed.) (2000) *Researching Language in Schools and Communities: Functional Linguistic Perspectives.* London: Cassell.

Van Ek, J. (1977) *The Threshold Level for Modern Language Learning in Schools.* London: Longman.

Van Lier, L. (1996) *Interaction in the Language Curriculum: Awareness, Autonomy and Authenticity.* London: Longman.

Ventola, E. (1987) *The Structure of Social Interaction: A Systemic Approach to the Semiotics of Service Encounters.* London: Pinter.

Vygotsky, L. (1968) *Thought and Language.* Cambridge, MA: MIT Press.

Webster, J. (2003–2009) *The Collected Works of M.A.K. Halliday, Volumes 1–10.* London: Continuum.

Webster, J. (2009) *The Essential Halliday: M.A.K. Halliday.* London: Continuum.

Wells, G. (1999) *Dialogic Inquiry: Toward a Sociocultural Practice and Theory of Education.* Cambridge: Cambridge University Press.

Wenger, E. (1998) *Communities of Practice: Learning, Meaning, and Identity.* Cambridge: Cambridge University Press.

White, B. and Custance, B. (2003) *Genre Mapping Across the Curriculum in SACSA.* South Australia: Catholic Education South Australia.

Widdowson, H. (1978) *Teaching Language as Communication.* Oxford: Oxford University Press.

Wilkins, D. (1976) *Notional Syllabuses.* Oxford: Oxford University Press.

Yalden, J. (1983) *The Communicative Syllabus: Evolution, Design and Implementation.* Oxford: Pergamon Press.